THE COMEBACK KIDS

TO JOE,

I HOPE IT'S NOT TOO PAINFUL READING. HOPE WE CAN GO TO A GAME IN FENWAY SOMETIME.

Steve Kaplan

THE COMEBACK KIDS

A Fan Relives the Amazing Baltimore Orioles 1989 Season

BY
STEVE KEPLINGER

Publishers Place
165 NORTH 100 EAST, ST. GEORGE, UTAH 84770, (801) 673-6333

To my mom, Betty, and my late grandmother, Anna Ruppert, who taught me to love the game, and to my wife, Jean, for never allowing me to give up.

CONTENTS

PREFACE

I am an Oriole fan. A dyed-in-the-wool, true blue, stick with them Birds, Oriole fan. First place or last place, 1988 or 1989, an Oriole fan. Therefore, if you are looking for an unbiased, clinical description of the Oriole franchise and the 1989 season, keep looking. This is not your book.

I am also a baseball fan, however, and consider myself a student of the game. I enjoy the intricacies and subtleties of baseball that do not exist in other sports. There is so much to watch, so much to take in, to fully appreciate the game. There are the battle of wits between pitcher and batter, the anticipation of a bunt by the third baseman, the perfect pitch for a hit-and-run, the unexpected suicide squeeze, and the time between each pitch to evaluate upcoming possibilities. Baseball is the chess game of team sports. It is the thinking person's game.

Baseball is therefore the kind of sport that demands introspection as well as retrospection. We will thus do just that, delving into the Oriole organization and the successes and failures that led to the incredible year of 1989. Only then can the magnitude of the 1989 Oriole season come into complete focus.

What I hope you will find is a combination of analysis and emotion, of facts and fervor, statistics and sentiment— which, of course, is what baseball is all about.

SO GIVE ME AN O....

—S.K.

CHAPTER ONE

More Than a Game

I was born with the Baltimore Orioles. While the move of the St. Louis Browns to Baltimore was being conceived, so was I. In 1954, the Baltimore Orioles were struggling through their first season, and I was struggling through my first year on earth. We grew up together, the Birds and I, learning and maturing with each passing year.

The Birds and baseball were always much more than a game to me. They were a part of my life from the beginning, an integral component in my day to day existence, not just a sport, you understand, but life and the best parts of life at that. The Birds were warmth, summer, outdoors. They were symbolic as well as tangible. Spring training meant that the dreaded winter would actually end, and we would return to those glorious days of summer and the warmth of Memorial Stadium, my second home.

Before I was old enough to attend school, my mom was rattling off to me the starting player at every position on every team in the American League. My grandmother was explaining the Charlie Lau theory of hitting to me before Charlie ever thought about being a coach. Each season in those early years, my grandad would bet on our hapless Orioles to win the pennant. Finally, in the Orioles' and my 13th year, he gave up and kept his money. That was the year the Birds took the Dodgers in four straight. In the important things, however, our family was much luckier. My mother's mom was the most avid Oriole fan I knew. She taught me more about baseball than everyone else combined, before or since. The doctors told us in 1963 that she had six months to live. What they did not realize is that my grandmom was not going anywhere until her beloved Orioles took that first crown. She was there three years later when the Birds took the "unbeatable" Los Angeles Dodger dynasty in four straight.

My first in-person Oriole game came when the Birds and I were five years old. Memorial Stadium was the grandest place I had ever seen. There, in the flesh, right in front of me was my team, the one I had seen on television and heard hundreds of times on the radio. I still remember parts of that game vividly. Best of all was the bottom of the eighth inning, a smack, an explosion of movement and noise, and a tiny sphere cutting through the smoke-filled sky and over the left field fence. Engulfed by people, my mom picked me up in time to see the flight of that ball into the night. The Birds may have finished in sixth place that year, 20 games out of first, but they won my first game when a 20-year-old pitcher named Milt Pappas hit his own three-run home run.

"Welcome to Memorial Stadium in Baltimore, Maryland...." The words themselves send chills up my spine to this day. The Birds' home. The Birds' only home. Since major league baseball returned to Baltimore, the Orioles have played every home game there. Over 2,700 baseball games in one of the best parks in baseball. Sentimental slop? Nostalgic overreaction? Perhaps. Admittedly, Memorial Stadium is part of my blood, part of myself. But after all, what is a stadium except memories? Thoughts of the great plays you have witnessed there, games you cannot forget, moments of your life that you will later recall as some of your best. If I had anything to do with it, the Birds would stay in Memorial Stadium forever. It, like Fenway Park and Wrigley Field, is packed with memories, but beyond that it is a very functional park. I've been to most stadiums in the country, and Memorial Stadium has to rank in the top three. Not only does the park itself boast one of the best fields in baseball, it is also comfortable for the fans. It sits in a quiet, residential neighborhood, with plenty of parking on and off the lot. There are literally hundreds of accesses to and from the ball yard, something almost no other stadium in the country can boast. The Orioles need a new antiseptic stadium in congested downtown Baltimore just slightly less than they do another team owner like the sanctimonious jackass that moved the Baltimore Colts out of town under the cover of night. I digress, however.

I think back to the Baby Birds of 1960, a group of kids so young many were not yet shaving. We were seven years old, the Birds and I. That year was our first taste of the other side of baseball, the winning side. The kids actually threatened to win the pennant, still in first place as late as Labor Day. But as usual, the Yankee dynasty won again. The damn Yankees. The hated Yankees. They always won, and I, like most Oriole fans, developed nearly as strong emotions for the Yanks as the Orioles. We hated them through and through. They were the consummate enemy. They represented a city we hated, a city of insensitive screamers, arrogant slobs, a city that outnumbered us in population ten to one. When New Yorkers considered Baltimoreans at all, they thought of us as bush-towners, uncultured, blue collar jerks. New Yorkers expected their team to win, and of course they did, year after year after year. That's what we hated the most. The Yankees always won. The rivalry was real, intense, and it spilled right onto the playing field. While no one in the remainder of the country knew anything about it, the nearly always second division Orioles and the nearly always first place Yankees fought a bitter rivalry. The Birds would beat the Yanks when they had no business beating anyone. Due much to those small successes in the early days, the Orioles remain to this day the team with the best overall record against the Bronx Bombers.

In 1964, the Birds were threatening again. But a great 97-65 season still left them two games behind the, you guessed it, damn Yankees. It was more of the same in 1965, close but still behind. We were a very good team, but we needed one more spark to be great. So we traded that pitcher who hit the home run in my first Oriole game for a guy named Frank Robinson. An "old 30" the Reds said when they made the trade. It is now often considered the most one-sided trade in the history of baseball. Frank went on to win the triple crown as the Birds blew away the American League. Oriole fans remained cautious however. It was not that we didn't have faith in our Birds, but we just didn't know quite what to do in this situation. Something could still go wrong, couldn't it? As 13 year olds, the Birds and I were full of energy and vigor. We spent the summer running in the 90 degree heat and 90% humidity of Baltimore and never broke a sweat. However, on Thursday afternoon, September 22, I found

16

myself perspiring profusely. Then, as Russ Snyder made that final catch to clinch the pennant, the sweat was replaced with a flood of emotions. I thought about my old friend Joey Sitko, a hated Yankee fan, and all the years I put up with him rubbing the Orioles' failure in my face, and felt fulfilled. I thought about my grandmom seeing this happen, and I started to cry. I also felt a deep sense of pride. The Birds and I had come a long way together, and I felt I was a literal part of this team. I had suffered with them, cried with them, and now I found myself celebrating with them.

From that point on, the Orioles became a great team, the dominant team in baseball in the late '60s and through the '70s. Pennant and/or division winners in '69, '70, '71, '73, '74, and '79, the Birds were a joy to watch. But even when they didn't win, they were always near the top, always finishing with a furious rush in September. They were great times. The best. The Orioles and I spent our formative years as winners in a class organization. Still, with all those thrills, there was never an emotional high quite as strong as the first time in 1966.

However, 1982 changed all that. The early '80s was the time of "Orioles Magic," the years when the Birds would pull out 20 or 30 games a year in the eighth and ninth inning, often at home. In 1982 Earl Weaver retired. It was also the height of the "Wild Bill" Hagy era and the screaming fans in section 34 in the upper deck of Memorial Stadium. It was an emotion-packed stadium every night. It was Rick Dempsey, the Orioles' catcher and spark plug, leading the fans in cheers. It was a city in love with a sports team and a team that loved its fans in return. It was a thrill a minute.

The Birds were falling just short in '82, however. As September arrived, it appeared that the Orioles were out of the hunt. They were overmatched by a number of teams in the American League East. Still, somehow, the Birds hung on by a thread. October arrived, and the Birds were coming home for a four game series versus the first place Milwaukee Brewers. The situation was simple. The Birds were three out with four games to play. They would need a four game sweep to capture the division. During the last two months of the season I had quietly secured tickets to all four of the remaining games, just on the off chance that this might happen. It did.

Games one and two were on Friday night. The emotion was intense. We all knew the odds were astronomical, but we also knew there was at least a possibility. The players knew it too, and as the game progressed you could see each player turn it up a notch higher than their normally high emotional pitch. By the end of the first game, we were all emotionally drained, but we won. Fortunately, we only had to wait 35 minutes for the next contest. No one could relax, however. Every warm-up pitch became high drama.

By the mid-innings it became clear that something was happening here. The bond between players and fans had always been strong in Baltimore, but this was different. Somehow, there seemed to be a direct line of adrenalin from the stands to the field. You could feel the excitment in your own body being metamorphosed into Oriole runs on the field. The Birds won again and people walked around town saying "Can you feel it?" and of course, you could.

On Saturday a cry echoed from the stadium that had been building each inning on Friday. "SWEEP! SWEEP! SWEEP! By the seventh inning you knew it was going to happen. The storybook finish would be set. The Birds had won three in a row. The American League East would be decided on the last day of the season.

Sunday finally came, bright and hopeful. Now, instead of just Baltimore and Milwaukee, the entire country was watching. The atmosphere was well beyond tense, something you could feel, but not quite explain. The Orioles fell behind early and continued to fall further behind. Before the late innings arrived, the game was over. We were not going to win this game. There would be no miracle today. The Birds were losing 10-2, but no one left the stadium. The game finally ended, still, no one left. The game had been over for 45 minutes, and the stadium was still full. Howard Cosell announced to a national television audience that he had never seen such a thing in sports. The Orioles were the losers, but their fans stayed, and they stayed, and they stayed. The players returned to the field, some still in uniform, some not. We stayed. We cheered. Rick Dempsey led the cheers one more time. Earl Weaver said thanks one more time. It was one of the most electric days of my life, and without question the most emotion I had ever experienced from a sporting event. Thinking back, I realize I felt more emotion that day than some people ever experience in their entire lives. I loved and respected a team of players and coaches, and that team loved and respected me back.

The next year, the Orioles were like a team possessed. They owed their fans something, as they saw it, and they did not let up until they had disposed of the Philadelphia Phillies in the World Series. It was a sweet victory, one I will always remember. But the pinnacle had come the year before. On that last day of the season we had lost a game, but learned the essence of sport. It is not winning or losing, or even how you play the game. It is camraderie and brotherhood, love and respect. It is a deep emotional bond that you will feel

19

forever. It is the essence of life.

In 1989, the Orioles returned to the elements of the game that made them great in the past. In one off season, Frank Robinson and Roland Hemond put together a squad of never-say-die kids. In one series their band of outfielders made more diving catches than the entire team did in 1988. This, combined with a staff of young arms that consistently threw strikes and an offense that did all the little things right, made Baltimore an immediate contender in the weak American League East. It was astounding to say the least.

My friends and acquaintances have little trouble understanding how I could follow that amazing team of comeback kids with such relish. What they could not understand is how or why I did the same thing in 1988, when the Orioles were the laughing stock of baseball, a team with 107 losses and the infamous 21-game losing streak.

I attempt to explain my relationship with the Orioles, our growing up together, the parallels in our lives. Then I mention that winning is great, but that sometimes losing is more important, more lasting, more impacting on our lives. Invariably, I receive a cold stare of incomprehension in return.

Somewhere, though, there are 51,642 people who sat in Memorial Stadium on one great October day who understand.

CHAPTER TWO

The Glory Years

As baseball teams go, the Baltimore Orioles are a young organization. At 35 years of age, many of their fans have been around longer than the team. Oh, of course, the franchise itself was originally the lowly St. Louis Browns. Perennial losers in the American League, the Browns had finished seventh or last in the league every season but one for the previous eight years. In 1948 they finished sixth, only 37 games out of first place. Whoopee. It's a wonder they were not banned from St. Louis. None of that mattered to Baltimore fans, however. The clock did not start for them until April 15, 1954, when that last place squad played their first game in Memorial Stadium and became the Baltimore Orioles.

Bob Maisel, the long time sports columnist for the *Baltimore Sun*, coined a phrase about Baltimore's new team that you heard often around town in those early years. "Last in hitting, last in pitching, last in the American League standings, but first in the hearts of Baltimore baseball fans."

It rang truer than even Bob Maisel would have guessed. The fans loved their team, despite their failures. When that first year had ended, however, the Orioles were not in last place; somehow Philadelphia managed that honor. Make no mistake, though, the Birds were bad. They lost 100 games that year. There was room for more than a little improvement, and improve they did, building from the bottom up, something that later was to become a Baltimore tradition, and its trademark in major league baseball.

Paul Richards was the manager in those early years of 1955 through 1961. Before the age of computer baseball and statistics on each batter versus left-handed pitchers on Saturday nights with the bases loaded and less than two outs, Richards was always thinking, always scheming. In 1956 Richards was platooning players, something that 20 years later would become common practice. He made a guy named Hoyt Wilhelm a starting pitcher at the tender age of 35. With his mystifying fingertip knuckleball, Wilhelm proceeded to no-hit the New York Yankee dynasty one fateful day in 1958. In the 30 plus years that have followed, the Yankees have never been no-hit again.

When his catchers could not find a way to snare Wilhelm's dancing pitch, Richards designed a bigger mitt. And while modern gloves bear little resemblance to those used in the '50s, Richards' mitt is an exception. Some catchers use virtually the same mitt today.

The next important step for the Birds came in the front office. Lee MacPhail, (later to become league president) was hired for the general manager post, and the tide began to turn for the organization.

By 1960, the league began to see the results of the new Oriole farm system. The "Baby Birds" were led by a 22-

year-old pitcher named Chuck Estrada and a 21-year-old named Steve Barber. In the field there was a 22-year-old rookie at shortstop named Ron Hansen who made the All-Star team. Over at third was the veteran Brooks Robinson, at 23 years of age. The kids stayed in first place much of the year, only to bow to the Yankees in a mid-September series. For the first time ever though, the Birds finished over .500 and out of the second division. Their 89-65 record took second place.

Baltimore continued the building process. They added pitchers like Milt Pappas and Wes Stock, infielders like Jerry Adair at second base, and outfielders like Russ Snyder. The long stretch of Jim Gentile anchored first base for the Birds. Diamond Jim was one of the most explosive hitters of his time. But, as always, his stats were buried under the Yankee powerhouses, and few people outside Baltimore even remember him. In Roger Maris' record 61 home run season of 1961, Gentile played in 13 fewer games but still outdid Maris in walks, doubles, RBI's, and slugging percentage.

There were more. A huge man named John Wesley Powell moved into the Oriole outfield, and later to first base replacing Gentile. Later, he became known simply as BOOG. Outside the organization, Lee MacPhail snatched Luis Aparacio, adding to what has become a long list of stellar defensive shortstops for the Birds. In the bullpen were guys like Dick "Turkey" Hall, and Stu Miller, a stopper who got opponents out not by blowing them away with heat, but by baffling them with an incredible variety of change-ups.

In 1964, the Birds threatened again. Featuring a stellar defense (95 total errors, lowest in baseball), and another rookie pitching sensation, Wally Bunker (who matched his 19 years on earth with wins), the Orioles were 97-65, only

23

two games behind the, you guessed it, New York Yankees.

The 1965 season produced virtually the same results. At 94-68 the Birds were a very good baseball team, but not good enough to win it all. It had also become obvious that the Oriole organization had swiftly become one of the best, if not the best, systems in baseball. That year the Orioles added Curt Blefary and Paul Blair, the Rookie of the Year center fielder. The farm system had also just produced another change of speed pitcher named Dave McNally. Incredibly, there was yet another 19-year-old pitcher who had just come up. Used mostly in relief in 1965, he was about to become the dominant pitcher in the American League for more than a decade to come. His name was James Alvin Palmer.

1965 was also Lee MacPhail's last year with Baltimore. Before leaving, however, he made one more trade: Milt Pappas and two players acquired earlier in the off season named Dick Simpson and Jack Baldschun for one Frank Robinson.

Frank, of course, went on to make that trade what is generally regarded as the most lopsided in baseball history. In 1966 he won the triple crown, hitting .316 with 49 home runs and 122 RBI's. Individual plays from that season have become permanent fixtures in my brain. May 8th, Mother's Day, at Memorial Stadium Frank Robinson connects with a Luis Tiant pitch, and the ball keeps soaring up and over the left field bleachers. The only ball ever hit completely out of Memorial Stadium. 23 years later a flag still waves at the very spot where the ball cleared the wall. A simple orange and black flag that has one word on it. The flag reads "HERE."

Then there was June 21st, Yankee Stadium. The dreaded Yanks are threatening in the bottom of the ninth. A drive to deep right field and Frank runs back to the short fence, leaps, and crashes into the stands. The fans molest Frank, pulling and shoving, but here he comes out, with the ball, and another Oriole win is preserved.

Frank added one more thing to this World Championship team—leadership in the form of laughs. In a kangaroo court, after every win, Frank the judge would fine players for bone-head plays or hot-dogging or anything else he could come up with. It brought the team closer together and loosened up the kids enough to play better baseball. Thus the last portion of the formula used to create the success of Oriole baseball was added.

After the Orioles had beaten the "unbeatable" L.A. Dodgers in four straight, including three shutouts thrown by Dave McNally, Jim Palmer, and Wally Bunker against the likes of Sandy Koufax and Don Drysdale, the building process continued. Frank Cashen and Harry Dalton were now making the player personnel decisions, but the tradition of excellence was just beginning. Another pitcher was brought up from the farm who became the Orioles' best hurler in 1967. In 1968, Tom Phoebus went on to throw a no-hitter. Next added was Mark Belanger, who only became the best defensive shortstop in the majors for years to come, winning eight gold gloves. Then there was Merv Rettenmund, another outfielder, who hit .322 for the Birds in 1970 and .318 in 1971. He is now the hitting instructor for the Kansas City Royals. They also added Don Buford from Chicago, who was to become the best lead-off hitter in Oriole history.

The talent did not stop on the field. The system was producing coaches just as quickly; coaches who in later years would be managing all over the majors. In 1968, the Birds brought up one of those coaches from the farm system, just like they did players. At the All-Star break he started managing. His name was Earl Weaver. Once again, all the pieces were in place: an impeccable defense, the best pitching staff in the majors, a clump of power hitters, and a feisty, statistics-oriented manager to lead them.

So as expected, 1969 proved to be an incredible year. This was arguably the best Oriole team ever, one of the best teams in this century. The club finished at 109-53, the nearest pursuer 19 games out. A pitching staff of screwballing Mike Cuellar (23-10), Dave McNally (20-7), Jim Palmer (16-4), and Tom Phoebus (14-7) tells much of the story. There were also four gold glove winners: Brooks at third, Belanger at short, Dave Johnson at second, and Paul Blair in center. Frank hit .308 with 100 RBI's, Boog Powell .304, with 121 RBI's. The Orioles made quick work of the Minnesota Twins in the first year of the championship series, sweeping them in three. But 1969 was the miracle year. The year the amazin' Mets somehow beat this powerful squad.

1970 was nearly a repeat of 1969. 108 wins instead of 109, the Birds won their last 11 regular season games this time. They then proceeded to sweep the Twins again in the championship series. This time, though, they went all the way, disabling the big Red Machine of Cincinnati four games to one.

1971 brought more of the same. The Orioles became only the third team in history to win 100 games or more, three years in a row. This was also the year of the four 20-game winners, Mike Cuellar, Pat Dobson, Dave McNally, and Jim Palmer. That had only happened one other time in the history of the sport. For the third year in a row the Birds swept the championship series, this time versus Oakland. They then lost to the Pittsburgh Pirates in the World Series in seven games.

In 1972, Oriole hitting fell off enough that the Birds fell five games short of first place. The pitching and defense remained its reliable self however, the team finishing with a 2.53 earned run average and two more gold gloves.

1972 also brought more talent from AAA Rochester. This time it was second baseman Bobby Grich, an International League MVP, and, of course, another excellent glove man. Then in 1973 the Birds added two more Rochester players. Al Bumbry, wearing number 1, batting number one, and Rich Coggins, wearing number 2, batting number two, wore out the basepaths. Bumbry hit .337, Coggins hit .319, and the defense and pitching just kept on coming. On top of that, another Baltimore product, Don Baylor, added more speed and big power. So just like that, the Birds were back in first place and into the playoffs.

1974 was the epitome of what Oriole baseball had become. Not a .300 hitter in the lineup, great all around defense, and pitching that got stronger while everyone else was fading in the heat of August and September. On August 28, the Birds were eight games out of first. But the furious pace to the wire, something fans were getting used to, occurred again. The Birds went 28-6 down the stretch, shutting out opponents for 54 straight innings at one point. They finished two games up on the Yankees to win yet another division title.

Another off season and more deals by Frank Cashen. First he got Lee May from Cincinnati to replace Boog Powell, a fixture at first for the last 14 years. Then in a virtual steal, Cashen got outfielder Ken Singleton and pitcher Mike Torrez from Montreal. May proceeded to knock in 99 runs, Singleton batted .300 and Torrez became a 20-game winner for the first time in his career. All of which still left the Birds 4 1/2 games out at the end of the '75 campaign. Another furious finish was not quite enough to make up for their poor start.

Before the '76 campaign started, the Orioles had an even more difficult task. Frank Cashen left baseball (later to return to make the Mets a powerhouse in the National League). Baltimore chose Hank Peters to fill the general manager position. Hank began with a bang...a big bang. His first trade brought Reggie Jackson to the Birds. Next, he made what became probably the second most important trade in Oriole history. He gave up Ken Holtzman, Grant Jackson, Elrod Hendricks, and Doyle Alexander to the Yankees for Dave Pagan, Rudy May, Rick Dempsey, Tippy Martinez, and Scott McGregor. Over the next 10 years, three of those players, Dempsey, Martinez, and McGregor, would play a major role in the success of the team. Not only were they good players, each fit the "Oriole mold" perfectly. Tough competitors, always giving everything they had, using every ounce of their ability, they inspired other Orioles, as well as the fans. Reggie Jackson though, was a different story. He contributed offensively, of course, but never seemed to quite fit in. He never seemed to be part of the emotionalism of the Orioles. The fans never accepted him.

Peters learned a valuable lesson. Talent was not all the Birds were looking for. Just as important was spirit and drive, comradery and emotion. The team concept and bond between players and fans had become an integral component in the Oriole success. It is said that people in Baltimore don't name candy bars after their favorite players, they name their children after them. So to many fans, the 1976 Orioles were not the Orioles at all. At 88-74, they finished 10 1/2 games

28

behind.

1977, and Reggie gone, the real Birds returned. Payrolls had skyrocketed in baseball with the advent of free agency. Not in Baltimore however. The team sported one of the lowest payrolls in baseball, but had one of their most successful seasons. Some people called them the "No-Names." But they went 97-65, tying for second in an extremely strong eastern division. They battled every game to the last out. Their fans loved them for it, and the emotion was back again. Newcomers? The Birds brought up another rookie from Rochester, a 21-year-old to do some designated hitting. He went on to be Rookie of the Year, and eventually the most prolific home run hitter in Oriole history. His name was Eddie Murray. In 1978, the Birds won 90 games again. But in the powerful eastern division of the American League, it was good enough only for fourth place.

So in 1979, the Birds made sure they could not be beat. They *never* lost a single series the entire year. They were the only team in the majors to win over 100 games. Oriole baseball, soon to be referred to as "Orioles Magic," was back. Another solid team with no stand-outs. Singleton, Murray, DeCinces, Dempsey, Pat Kelly, Terry Crowley, Roenicke, Lowenstein, Flanagan, McGregor, and on and on. Almost as important as the players were a bunch of rowdy individuals in section 34 of the upper deck led by one "Wild Bill" Hagy, spelling out O-R-I-O-L-E-S with contortions of his rather rotund anatomy. They had cheers for every Oriole. Ken Singleton would come up and the roar would come from section 34, "HEY KEN, PUT ONE IN THE BULLPEN!" Then Murray would stride to the plate, and the rythmic chant would start, "ED-DIE! ED-DIE!"

The Orioles took out the Angels in the championship

series before bowing to the Pirates yet again in the seventh and final game of the Series.

The Birds were just as good in 1980, in some ways better. It was Steve Stone's incredible Cy Young season, going 25-7. The club had the highest team batting average in its history (.273). The O's won 100 games again...and came in second in the best division in baseball.

The strike shortened season of 1981 took the guts out of a team that won by wearing down its opponents in a long season pennant drive. The Birds were two games back in both the first and second halves of that strange year.

All of which brings us back to that grand year of 1982, the 33-10 rush to the finish by the O's, and that grand emotion of the last day of the season. The O's took their third world championship the following year, closing out one of the most amazing stretches in sports history.

From 1960 through 1983, the Birds of Baltimore completely dominated major league baseball. During those 24 years they were 612 games over .500, playing at a .581 pace. Their closest competitor of the era, the New York Yankees, was 99 1/2 games behind. The Orioles finished first eight times, won six American League pennants, and three World Series. They finished second eight times. Only twice in this 24-year period did the Birds finish below .500. They also won 47 Gold Gloves, highest in the American League. They produced 22 20-game winners, a record that no one is remotely close to in the history of baseball.

They did all this by 1) building the strongest farm system in the game; 2) always stressing defense and pitching first; 3) making a minimum number of trades to add a missing element to an already strong team; 4) utilizing players who did not necessarily lead the league, but performed in the clutch; and 5) relying on the team concept using "team" players who got the most from their own ability and were able to play at a high emotional pitch. Simple.

CHAPTER THREE

What Happened?

As history shows, the Orioles steadily declined after the 1983 World Championship. In fact, they are one of only four teams in major league history to have progressively worse records in five successive years. Trying to ascertain exactly what happened to the Oriole organization is not an easy task. Even for those watching the team on a daily basis, it was difficult to tell exactly what went wrong.

Outwardly, things did not appear that much different. For the most part, the same pitchers seemed to be taking the mound and the same hitters came to the plate. In addition, the O's kept adding more hitters each year. What happened?

To find our first clue, it is necessary to backtrack to the 1980 season. That was the first year that Edward Bennett Williams, the renowned Washington, D.C., attorney, had taken over full ownership of the ball club. It was during Mr. Williams' tenure that a philosophical change took place in the organization's approach. EBW did much to help the Oriole cause. First and foremost, he built an even larger base of fan support, increasing the Birds' geographical appeal by drawing fans from D.C., Virginia, and North Carolina on a regular basis. Because of this, attendance improved dramatically in Baltimore. From 1980 through 1988, Bird annual attendance averaged just under 1,800,000, even though the last five years of this period were some of the worst in Oriole history. Before Williams, home attendance averaged just over 1,000,000 per year.

Williams wanted an Oriole winner more than anyone. This, however, became part of the problem as we will see. In addition, he was willing to spend money to keep his ballplayers, something that seemed mandatory during this age of free agency. But even though the Birds had lost some great talent to free agency since it began in 1976, they kept winning through it all. Now here's Edward Bennett Williams willing to spend money to keep such Orioles, and get some new ones, and the Birds start losing. What gives?

Next, there was the coaching base. Much of the Oriole success in the farm system, and eventually in the majors must be attributed to the strength of the coaching staff throughout the organization. As the '70s rolled on, the rest of baseball began to see all this talent. So, one by one, Baltimore coaches were plucked out of the organization and given jobs as managers or coaches somewhere else. Joe Altobelli, George Bamberger, Jim Frey, Billy Hunter, Ray Miller, and Frank Robinson all left the big league club to take jobs elsewhere. Earl Weaver retired. More coaches from the minor league levels were snatched. This drain of coaching talent took its toll and caught up with the Birds in 1984.

At the major league level the Orioles were still respectable in 1984. But that was the season the Tigers won 35 of their first 40 games, making a shambles of the Eastern Division pennant race before it ever began. The O's finished 85-77, 19 games back. Injuries decimated the squad, so fans were not overly concerned about their team coming apart at the seams. But by season's end, Jim Palmer, Al Bumbry, and Ken Singleton had all left the team. Palmer and Singleton retired, while Bumbry played one final year with San Diego. It was hard to imagine the Orioles without them, and this time there was no one coming up to fill their shoes.

The Birds had big holes to fill, and the way the organization saw it, there was no choice but to go out and fill them. John Lowenstein left early in the '85 campaign, and the holes got bigger. So Hank Peters went out and added some new life to the Bird lineup: Fred Lynn from California, Lee Lacy from Pittsburgh, and Alan Wiggins from San Diego. And while the Oriole record in '85 was much the same as '84 (83-78, 16 games out), this was the year that changed Oriole baseball. When the O's won, they won in a different way than they had in the past. There were more and more high scoring games, Oriole fielding was no longer number one, and the team ERA went from 3.71 to 4.38. Complete games dropped from 48 to 32, and shutouts went from 13 to six.

The O's were replacing fleet-footed centerfielders Al Bumbry and John "T-Bone" Shelby with a slow Freddy Lynn who was not reaching anything in the power alleys. Next to Lynn they put a below average fielder, Lee Lacy. Inexplicably, the Birds replaced the arguably best defensive second baseman in the American League, Rich Dauer, with a guy named Alan Wiggins. Alan was the complete opposite of the "Oriole player." He had a past history of drug problems; he made an inordinate amount of mental errors in the field and on the basepaths, and his physical errors were not far behind. All this in the name of more offense, and more offense is exactly what they got. They scored more runs, hit more home runs, had more total bases, and hit for a higher slugging percentage than any time in Oriole history. Did it win more games? No. Worse, the organization somehow set about to solve the problem by adding *more* offense. Next, EBW spent some more money and lured Earl Weaver out of retirement. Earl was back, but he could not play second base, and he could not replace his old buddy Jim Palmer on the mound.

Here came 1986, and the Orioles were disregarding everything they could have learned from themselves over the past 30 years. They fielded much the same team they did in '85, thinking that Weaver was going to turn everything around. In addition, Dauer was gone, as were Gary Roenicke (the right-handed side of the best platoon left field had ever seen), and Wayne Gross, who had added some much needed stability to third base.

They gave up on Dennis Martinez, the pitcher on the staff who always had the most "stuff," but never seemed to be able to put it all together. They replaced him with Ken Dixon, another pitcher with a good fastball, but who had a propensity for giving up the gopher ball.

Give up the long ball is exactly what Dixon did, too. So, in fact, what the Orioles ended up doing in '86 was weaken their defense and their pitching even more. They put Larry Sheets in the outfield for 32 games, making what was already a slow group downright leaden. At third base they played no less than *ten* people. Floyd "Sugar Bear" Rayford, Juan Bonilla, Juan Beniquez, Tom O'Malley, Jackie Gutierrez, Ricky Jones, Rex Hudler, Tom Dodd, Kelly Paris, and yes, believe it or not, even Larry Sheets. They combined to make

40 errors. Rayford played the position more than anyone. He was a likable fellow that you could not help but root for, but his rotund shape made it impossible for him to play the kind of defense the Birds had so long taken for granted.

Still, on August 6, the Birds were only 2 1/2 games out of first, and it appeared Weaver was working some sort of miracle. After all, the O's are always hot down the stretch, right? Wrong! This team bore no resemblance to Oriole teams of the past. This was a team that relied strictly on the hit, the kind of team that fades down the stretch, rather than the kind that turns it on like the old Orioles. The '86 Birds looked more like the Red Sox teams of the '70s. Plenty of sticks and nothing else. So the Birds, like all those Red Sox teams, faded and faded and faded, losing 42 of their last 56. They finished 73-89 and for the first time in Oriole history, a last place team.

Then came 1987, and it was obvious to all that the Baltimore Orioles had big problems. Cal Ripken, Sr., a forever Oriole coach, got his shot at managing. He had given more of himself to the Oriole organization than any other individual. He certainly deserved the opportunity.

Hank Peters went out looking for more help swinging more of EBW's money in the air, but everyone seemed to be missing the problem. He landed Ray Knight from the New York Mets to fill the huge hole at third base. Ray Knight, another good hitter, got everyone's mouth watering. WOW! What a lineup! But Knight was, at best, a below average defensive third baseman. They got Rick Burleson to play second, still a good hitter, but average defensively, due to a previously injured arm. Then came what some consider, including myself, the death blow. The Orioles traded Storm Davis, a 24-year-old pitcher in the mold of Jim Palmer who led the starters in ERA in 1986, to San Diego for relief pitcher Mark Williamson and catcher Terry Kennedy. The O's then let long time spark plug and strong defensive catcher Rick Dempsey go.

Kennedy, of course, added more offense for the Birds. His defense however was atrocious, at least compared to what Oriole fans were accustomed. Now, not only did the Orioles have an agonizingly slow outfield and erratic defense at second and third, they now had a catcher that the league began stealing bases on like a Chinese fire drill. At the same time they gave up their best ERA pitcher. As if things were not bleak enough, the Birds gave up on their best defensive outfielder, John "T-Bone" Shelby, because he was not hitting. He was traded to the Dodgers for relief specialist, Tom Niedenfuer, who was in Manager Tommy Lasorda's doghouse and was not playing anyway. To top off the entire situation, it appeared to fans as if long time favorite Eddie Murray was "dogging it" in the field. Balls were skipping past him that he always seemed to stop in previous years. Finally the owner made some comments about Eddie's effort, and Murray's heart never again seemed to be in an Oriole game.

Now with this picture painted, you might assume that the Orioles knew they were in for a long year. On the contrary, everything was upbeat, and the organization fully expected with even more *offense* the Birds would turn things around. The offense came through once again. The Birds were hitting long balls in droves, 211 in total. Balls were flying out of Memorial Stadium like no one had ever seen. Unfortunately for Bird fans, they were flying out for both teams. The O's ERA ballooned to 5.01. The Birds finished 67-95, 31 games out of first.

There was no hiding anymore. This was a bad team. The O's had fallen into the same trap as many other major league clubs. Spend lots of money; keep your players happy; make the quick fix by landing some free agents; get more hitters, more explosion, more power.

What they found out is what they really knew already, and what diehard Oriole fans certainly knew. There is no quick fix. Teams are not happier when individual players are making huge globs of money, and defense and pitching win baseball games.

It was time to bite the bullet. It was time to get back to Oriole baseball. It was time to rebuild from the bottom, get back to defense, and slowly bring back the team concept. With that commitment made, the Orioles knew it would be a long haul back to a competitive squad at the major league level. They knew the next four, maybe five years, would be very lean. They also knew, though, that it had to be done. To get there, the organization and fans would have to suffer through the incredibly embarrassing year of 1988.

CHAPTER FOUR

The Disaster Year

The Orioles were making major changes during the 1988 season behind the scenes: new personnel in the player development office, new coaches at the minor league level, new minor league scouts, new spring training facilities, a new conditioning coach. The Birds seemed finally to be moving in the right direction again, but no one would see anything positive at the major league level in 1988. Nothing.

1988 was absolutely and positively the worst year in Oriole history. Period. Everyone in the country, including those not the least bit interested in baseball, knew just how bad the Orioles were. Nationally syndicated cartoons poked fun at the Birds all spring. One showed Charlie Brown, triumphant, finally winning a baseball game. "WE WON! WE WON!" he yelled.

Lucy then responds, "Calm down, Charlie Brown, it was just the Orioles."

There were jokes making the rounds from Key West to Olympia. The one about the child in custody court, who did not want to be placed with either parent, was typical. "Please don't send me to my father, he beats me. Don't send me to my mother either, she also beats me."

"Then where am I to send you?", the judge asks.

"Send me to the Orioles, they never beat anybody."

A national television sports show ran a graphic each day of the baseball season comparing the Orioles' progress with that of the 1962 New York Mets, generally regarded as the worst team in baseball history. Even the *Baltimore Sun* got into the act, matching up the '62 Mets and '88 Birds on a computer. (The Orioles won the re-enactment, but just barely.)

Could the Birds really be as bad as all that? A team with two genuine superstars in Cal Ripken, Jr. and Eddie Murray? Say it ain't so. But it was so. They were that bad, maybe worse.

You cannot start a discussion of the '88 O's without quickly mentioning "THE STREAK." "THE STREAK," for those of you living under a rock during the calendar year of 1988, began with day one of the season. It ended 22 games later. Previous to "THE STREAK," the Birds' worst start was in 1978 when they lost their first five games. Bird fans were used to the Orioles getting off to a slow start. This, however, went way beyond the worst nightmare of the biggest pessimist in the state of Maryland. The 21-game streak established the major league record for consecutive losses starting a season. It also set the American League record for the longest losing streak ever. Mercifully, it fell two short of the major league record held by the infamous '61 Phillies. Thank you, Philadelphia. During "THE STREAK" the Orioles were outscored 129 to 44. They hit .200 while their opponents hit .311. The Orioles' ERA was a cool 5.96 compared to the opponents' 1.93.

After the first six games of "THE STREAK," Oriole management felt a need to do something, anything. So Cal Ripken, Sr. was replaced at the helm by Frank Robinson. Fans were dismayed. Cal, Sr. was an integral part of Oriole baseball. Not only had he given much of his life to the organization, he had also given the team two of his sons. The Ripkens were long-time Maryland residents, one of the most respected and well-known families in the state. The losses were bad enough. Now the most important sports family in town was being ripped apart. These were not happy times. Could things get any more miserable? You bet they could. Poor Cal, Jr. and Billy, already suffering enough, now had a much heavier burden. Billy seemed especially demoralized by the firing. His average went from .308 in '87 to .207 in '88. After his dad was gone, Billy promptly had his uniform number changed to his father's.

So while the fans suffered with the Ripkens, they knew that something had to be done. Frank Robinson, always popular in Baltimore, was the best guy for the job in most fans' eyes. After managing stints in Cleveland and San Francisco, Frank had rejoined the Orioles as a coach in 1985. Before the '88 season had begun, Frank was moved to the front office as a special assistant to Roland Hemond, the general manager. Robbie was obviously being groomed for the general manager position, himself. But when things turned from bad to terrible on the field, Edward Bennett Williams promptly asked Frank if he would mind turning in his coat and tie for a uniform. The relationship between EBW and Frank had grown close over the years, and he was happy to oblige. While Frank knew beforehand that this was not going to be fun, he never dreamed just how dreadful it

43

would be. His team proceeded to lose another 15 straight games before he would finally see them victorious in Chicago on April 29.

His team went on to have six four-game losing streaks and another five-game streak. His longest winning streak of the entire year would be four. Never during the season would his team win a single series in an American League Eastern Division ballpark. He would use 43 different players during the year and 127 different lineups. That was just the beginning, however.

Baltimore fans, for the most part, handled all this relatively well. They were not used to this kind of embarrassment, but they learned to roll with the punches quickly. During "THE STREAK," fans drove around Baltimore all day with their lights on, an outward symbol of the bond between fans and team. A disc jockey named Bob Rivers vowed midway through "THE STREAK" that he would stay on the air until the Orioles won. Fortunately, he worked on an FM station that played sections of albums, allowing him to catch cat-naps during songs. He would need them as he spent the next 11 straight days on the radio. On another Baltimore radio station, sports commentator "Stan the Fan" came to work adorned in hair curlers and a dress. Stan announced, "I want to show what a drag losing is." Housewives pledged to "withhold marital favors" until the Birds won. Obviously, these were desperate times.

Finally, the Birds won that first game, and they were headed home. It was May 2, the second month of the season, and the Orioles had won a total of one game. They had just suffered through the worst month in modern major league history. How many people could possibly show up to see a 1-21 baseball team? 2,000? 6,000? How about 50,402 yelling, screaming fans welcoming their team home. It was an uplifting experience for a downtrodden team, something that would buoy them through a season worse than any of them could imagine. The O's won their second that night, 9-4. The fans kept coming, too. By season's end, the O's had drawn 1,660,738, a miraculous total for a team that was not only bad, but out of the pennant race since day one. There was never a reason for anyone to come to the park, at least not that outsiders could see. But they were there, and the players did not forget it.

Why were the Orioles so incredibly deficient? This time the answer was hitting. After all, the Birds pitching and defense had already collapsed well before the '88 season. This new Oriole squad of the last four years relied on hitting. The reason they therefore went from a bad team to one of the worst in baseball history was the loss in sticks. Not only was their .238 average the team's lowest since 1972, it was also the American League's lowest since 1982. They managed to score just 550 runs, matching the second lowest total in the AL in 16 years. Cal and Eddie combined to knock in or score nearly half of the Oriole runs. After them, the offense was beyond anemic. No one on the club hit as high as .290, and no one but Cal and Eddie hit 20 or more extra base hits in any category. It was too early for any of the Oriole moves toward stronger defense and pitching to pay off yet. All they managed to do was weaken themselves offensively.

Defense remained much the same as in '86 and '87—poor, at best. The O's made 119 errors, tied for seventh in the AL. While this may not seem terrible to some teams, it was the third time in the last four years that the Birds did not finish in the top three in the league. The team had finished in the top three 22 times in the previous 25 years. Worse than the

45

errors, however, were the plays the O's just could not make, especially in the outfield. Their range was extremely limited, and Oriole fans would be hard pressed to remember a single ball run down in either power alley until the final month of the season. This lack of speed and agility probably cost the team 20 games by itself. In the infield, the Birds remained erratic at first and third. Eddie Murray's defense continued to slide. His 11 errors were second worst in the league. In addition, he failed to make the plays he would easily have turned into outs five years ago. It also became obvious to the Birds that Rick Schu was not the answer at third.

The few bright spots included Billy Ripken's stellar play at second. Cal was his reliable self at short. A cast-off catcher let go by the Oakland A's showed some promise behind the plate. His name—Mickey Tettleton.

Team pitching also bore a strong resemblance to the last two years. Team ERA was 4.54, lower than in '87, but still the highest in the majors. The O's also were worst in the majors in runs allowed (789) and batting average against (.274!).

As if the horrendous 54-107 season was not bad enough, Oriole fans had more pain coming. In July, there would be much more than the loss of baseball games to suffer. Ralph Salvon, the Orioles' trainer, seemingly forever, would pass away unexpectedly after complications from heart surgery. Ralph was always much more than a trainer for the Birds. Ralph was the guy players commiserated and laughed with, the guy they went to for mental as well as physical well-being. Ralph Salvon was as recognizable to Oriole fans as any player, and just as much a part of the team. Now Ralph, a symbol of the Oriole spirit, was gone. August came and the tragedy continued. The Birds' owner, Edward Bennett

Williams, died after a long bout with cancer. There seemed to be no end to the pain of 1988.

But finally, mercifully, the season ended. The collapse of the Orioles was now complete. When the Oriole bats fell silent, there was absolutely nothing left. No hitting, no pitching, no defense. In hindsight, maybe the organization should have seen this coming. Maybe they knew it was coming.

But in the end, all that was left was a skeleton of a baseball team, dejected, demoralized, and broken.

CHAPTER FIVE

The Winter of Our Discontent

T he season was over and I, like most Bird fans, found myself in a deep funk. As the days passed, though, the pain subsided, and slowly it was replaced first by pride and then by optimism. Pride in a last place team? Optimism, you say? That, of course was exactly the reaction of those around me. A well-founded reaction, I must say. I was surrounded by non-Oriole fans, and mostly non-baseball fans. Most of those people, knowing me as a strange enough character to begin with, thought I had finally gone completely insane. When I proudly wore my Oriole jacket everywhere I went, patiently explaining to snickering passers-by that my team would be back, they usually broke into hysterical laughter. The sound still echoes in my ears. The Oriole paraphernalia decorating my office was randomly defaced by fellow workers, the word "Orioles" being replaced by the name of a cookie with black outsides and white filling. "O's" was replaced with "Zer-O's."

I could take it though. It was obvious to me that the Oriole organization had made the commitment to rebuild this team the right way. They were working hard at the minor league levels, and they were stressing pitching and defense. Eventually, the Orioles I had known and loved for all those years would be back. How long would it take? *Quien sabe?* But I knew I could take it until we were competitive again, and it would be great fun watching us get there.

My optimism had actually begun during the dreaded season, believe it or not. In July, the Orioles had already started planning for the future at the major league level. The first question that had to be answered in that pursuit was, "Is there any talent already here good enough to build a new team around?" The answer was obvious to both fans and management. Cal Ripken, Jr. was soon to turn 28, still young enough to be a major factor when the Birds became competitive again. Cal was not only steady in the field and at the plate, he was also a steadying influence on the younger players. He was a leader and a perfect role model for the rest of the team. Was there anyone else on this team with too much talent to let go, and still young enough to be a factor in four to five years? Probably not.

With that decision made, the Birds signed Cal to a three year contract. That day, July 27, marked the unofficial beginning of the Orioles' off-season, though there were still two months to go of "playing out the string." Roland Hemond knew that the teams in the midst of a pennant race were going to be desperate for immediate talent for their stretch runs. He would be only too happy to oblige, for the right price, and the right price was young talent, especially pitchers and strong defensive players.

On July 30, I became convinced that the Birds were moving in the right direction. I also knew that this was not

50

going to be a painless process. The Birds traded Mike Boddicker, their best pitcher over the last five years, to the Boston Red Sox. Mike was the consummate Oriole, a crafty change of speed pitcher with pinpoint control. He loved Baltimore and its fans, and his emotional speech before his departure left me in tears. But I knew that it had to be done. And when I saw our portion of the trade, 24-year-old Brady Anderson, running around in centerfield like a gazelle, making diving catches like I had not seen from an Oriole in six years, I was sure we had done the right thing. In addition, the Orioles added another pitcher in the deal, 21-year-old Curt Schilling. It was obvious that Curt was not ready for the majors, but what raw talent!

Before the season ended, Hemond pulled off two more trades. The first sent the Orioles' professional pinch hitter, Jim Dwyer, to Minnesota for another young pitcher, Doug Kline. Then on the last day of August, Fred Lynn was dealt to the Tigers for more young talent, catcher Chris Hoiles and pitchers Robinson Garces and Cesar Mejia. All were at least a year away from the majors, but we were stockpiling young pitchers and defensive talent. I, for one, was a happy Oriole fan.

Meanwhile, back on the farm, things were developing nicely, and my optimism continued to grow. The Birds had signed 17 of their top 20 draft picks in '88. Their AAA farm team, the Rochester Red Wings, finished in first place with the club's best record since 1976. Johnny Oates, a former Oriole catcher, was manager of the Red Wings and was selected Manager of the Year in the International League. Craig Worthington, the club's third baseman, was named the league's Most Valuable Player, due much to his outstanding defense at the hot corner. Steve Finley, a 23-year-old outfielder, who vaulted from A ball earlier in the year to AAA, batted .314, ran down everything in the outfield near him, and was named Rookie of the Year. In addition, there were a host of pitchers showing promise. Among them were Pete Harnisch and Bob Milacki, both brought up by the O's in September. Harnisch was chosen by *Baseball America* as the number one prospect in the AA Southern League, while pitching for Charlotte. Milacki stunned Oriole fans by going 2-0 in three starts for the Birds, pitching to a 0.72 ERA.

This was getting exciting. The next step, right after the season ended, made me smile even more. Frank Robinson needed his own coaching staff, guys that he felt comfortable with, and people who espoused the old Oriole philosophy, which had just become the new Oriole philosophy. He also needed teachers, guys who knew their trade inside and out and would be patient with a young, aggressive squad that he hoped to put together. Three days after the season ended, Frank named his first replacement. Cal Ripken, Sr. would be back with the Orioles, coaching third base. In what could have been an impossible situation for many people, Cal graciously accepted and was back with the Oriole family, where he belonged. I felt an immediate upsurge of spirit and knew the Birds would be a better team in '89, based simply on this one move.

Frank was not finished though. For the first base coaching job he stayed within the organization choosing the International League's Manager of the Year, Johnny Oates. Next Frank chose Tom McCraw as hitting instructor. McCraw had worked with Frank before in both Cleveland and San Francisco. McCraw left the Mets organization as a roving hitting instructor to join his friend Frank in rebuilding the Birds. With him came Frank's choice for pitching coach, Al

Jackson. While Frank had no previous experience with Jackson, his philosophy seemed to mirror that of the "Old Orioles" and Frank himself. "Throw strikes, get ahead in the count, make the batter hit the ball, and don't walk anyone." His success with Met pitchers was not bad testimony either.

That behind them, Hemond and Robinson concentrated on the team. First, they cut loose those who were either not contributing, or too old to fit in the youth movement. Don Aase, the stopper with arm problems, was gone. Doug Sisk, a reliever who allowed 22 of the 49 runners he inherited to score, was gone. Jeff Stone, a "stone" in the Oriole outfield, was gone. Tom Niedenfuer was lured away by Seattle in the free agent market. Fans were disappointed by the Niedenfuer signing only because they would no longer get to see his wife, actress Judy Landers, in the stands.

The Birds signed some players of their own. Mickey Weston, who had pitched to a 2.09 ERA in the Mets system, and Tim Hulett, a utility infielder who had played previously with the White Sox, were inked. They traded Doug Kline to Montreal for a fireballing 28-year-old named Michael Anthony Smith. Then they acquired another pitcher from Cincinnati named Michael Anthony Smith. In spring training they would become known as "Mississippi Mike" and "Texas Mike," respectively, so people could tell them apart. Another trade, sending minor league pitcher Peter Blohm to the Pirates, brought the O's first baseman Randy Milligan. Milligan had only 82 at bats in the majors, but Baltimore obviously saw some potential that Pittsburgh did not. The fact that the Orioles traded for a first baseman convinced me that the move I felt was mandatory would occur.

In a few more weeks, at the winter meetings in Atlanta, it

happened. Eddie Murray, the all time Oriole home run hitter, the guy described by the *Elias Baseball Analyst* as "the quintessential clutch-hitter of the past decade," was traded to the L.A. Dodgers. It had to be done. The Birds had no choice for a number of reasons. First, Eddie was 33 years old. It would be unlikely that he could be a contributor when the Orioles became competitive again. Second, Eddie's $2 million salary was draining the organization of money it should be spending on young talent. Third, Eddie had stopped performing to his best abilities in Baltimore. The fact that he was not putting forth maximum effort on the field was a detriment to the team concept of the Orioles. So while his offense would be missed immensely, his attitude, to say the least, would not be an example for the younger players that would surround him.

In return, the O's got pitchers Brian Holton and Ken Howell, plus slick fielding shortstop Juan Bell, the brother of George Bell. If the trade had stopped there, it might not have been a very good one for the Birds. But they then traded Ken Howell and minor league pitcher Gordon Dillard to the Phillies for outfielder Phil Bradley. Bradley, considered by some to be the best defensive outfielder in the National League, would help the O's tremendously, especially if he could hit near his lifetime .293 average. Now I was really getting excited.

Two more trades would also be instrumental for the Birds. The first sent catcher Terry Kennedy to San Francisco for catcher Bob Melvin. The new Oriole philosophy was again evident here. They traded away some offense for a much better defensive catcher. Then during spring training, the O's landed a guy they originally wanted in the Eddie Murray trade, Mike Devereaux. Devereaux was another fleet-footed outfielder who had hit .340 at AAA Albuquerque in 1988. To get him, the Birds traded pitcher Mike Morgan, a guy who did not fit in the Oriole plans at all for 1989.

When all was said and done, it appeared the O's had improved themselves substantially in defense, even at the major league level. They had possibly improved their pitching slightly. Their offense, though seemingly impossible, appeared to be even weaker than last year. They certainly had added a host of youthful talent for the future. It would be three to four years before we knew for sure. I, however, was chomping at the bit now. It was January, but I wanted to see what these guys could do. Enough winter, let's get this season going! To keep myself occupied, I sat at home charting players, deciding for myself who would and would not make this team, devising batting orders, developing a starting rotation and a bullpen, wondering if Frank could use my help.

One day, during the eternal month of January, I was in Las Vegas. While everyone else in the sports book was quietly choosing their basketball picks, I was studying the odds chart for the 1989 pennant and World Series. There, right at the very bottom of the list, was my beloved team.

	To win the Pennant	To win the World Series
Baltimore Orioles	150-1	300-1

What?! Are you crazy? My Orioles? Suddenly, the 1988 season flashed through my head. I had almost forgotten just how bad....Realism set in. But the words came out of my mouth anyway, "Oh well, what do they know?"

CHAPTER SIX

The Grand Tryout Camp

Febuary 16, 1989. In Sarasota, Florida, at the Orioles' brand new training facility, Twin Lakes Park, 29 potential major league pitchers and catchers have gathered. One week later they are joined by 24 more prospects. Before it is over, two more possibilities enter the mix.

It is 1989 now. No one can make the agony of '88 disappear, but it is now officially the past. It is springtime in Florida, the season of beginnings, of new life, of starting over. New, in fact, is the key word for the Baltimore Orioles. There is a new training facility, new coaches, new players, a new attitude, even new uniforms, which will not be unveiled until opening day.

The task ahead looks formidable, to say the very least. With a record number of players here, this year's Oriole spring training looks more like a tryout camp. Most major league teams will be spending the next five weeks getting into shape, with a battle for one, maybe two positions in the field. In addition, maybe there will be a choice to make for the fifth starter on the squad.

In the Birds' camp however, anything could happen at any position on the field. Of the 53 players in camp, only four have guaranteed spots. Cal Ripken and Phil Bradley will play somewhere in the infield and outfield respectively. What position will either play? No one knows. On the pitching staff, Dave Schmidt and Brian Holton are assured of spots on the team. Brian however, has no idea whether he will start, be the closer, or pitch middle or long relief.

There are kids everywhere. The average age on the major league roster is 26 (youngest in baseball). Twenty-six of the 38 players on this roster have less than two years of major league experience. There is not a single pitcher in camp who has won 15 games in the majors. Only one player, Larry Sheets, has ever hit 30 home runs in a season, and that happened only one year, in what is now being regarded as a fluke. Only three players on the roster have ever driven in 50 runs in the majors.

What a job. The task ahead is so herculean it boggles the imagination. No one is looking for an escape hatch, however. This is going to be a long, hard climb. Frank Robinson, for one, is ready for it.

"Last year," he says, "I let the players do things their way. I saw some good things and some bad things. I got to gauge some things. This year, we're going to do things my way." Where in the world do you start with so much to accomplish in so short a time? "Fundamentals," Frank says, adding immediately, "I know, I know. Every manager says that. But we're definitely going to do it. We're going back to the basics. We're going to work hard, very hard," another famous manager cliche. "But I mean it," Robinson says. "We're going to work on bunting, on hitting-and-running.

You watch."

So we watch. And of course, he does mean it. These little Birds are running all over the field, bunting, sacrificing, hitting behind runners, stealing, hitting-and-running. It has been so long since Oriole fans have seen their team hit behind a runner, some cannot believe this is the O's. By March, the Birds are doing lots of little things they never managed to do in 1988. The new outfielders are stealing second and then third base. There are sacrifice flies and sacrifice bunts. Manufactured runs. Only an Oriole fan could appreciate how exciting it is to see the Birds score a run on one hit. Maybe this team will not score much, and probably they will finish last again, but this is exciting to watch, and it is obvious that this team is finally moving in the right direction.

It is also becoming obvious that this is a different Frank Robinson we are watching. Frank has suddenly become a hands-on manager. He is upbeat, motivational, patient. He is more personal with the players, laughing and having fun. No longer is he expecting his players to perform to his own Hall of Fame standards. Frank is changing his approach to match his young and inexperienced squad. It is amazing how patient he has become after watching his team lose 107 games last year.

So while the players are learning a new philosophy and practicing and practicing their fundamentals, intense battles are taking place for spots on the team. The big experiment involves the 20-year-old rookie obtained in the Eddie Murray deal, Juan Bell. Juan shows great range as a shortstop, and an even better arm. The jury is still out on his ability to hit major league pitching, however. Will the Birds move Cal Ripken to third, and put Juan at short? Most feel sure that will be the case, feeling the O's must justify the Murray trade, and anyway, what did a team coming off a 107-loss season have to lose? In the end, though, the Birds feel Bell will be hurt by bringing him to the majors at this early stage of his career. Instead, they will put Craig Worthington on third, the International League MVP, and leave Cal at short. There are questions about Worthington's hitting also, but there are no doubts about his glove. Craig will indeed be the Birds' best defensive third baseman in years, and defense is utmost in Frank Robinson's mind.

Another battle is raging at first base, where the O's have the minor problem of replacing roughly one-fourth of last year's offense in Eddie Murray. Larry Sheets has lost 30 pounds in his attempt to land the job, and escape his solitary role as designated hitter. Jim Traber, the Columbia, Maryland boy, has lost 15 pounds himself. Randy Milligan, the new arrival from the Pirates says he cannot see himself not winning the job. All that is before the O's invite a fourth possibility to camp, home run clouting Bob Horner. Bob is attempting to make a comeback from the shoulder injury that sidelined him most of 1988 with the St. Louis Cardinals. While the Orioles are aware of Horner's propensity for getting injured, he is not an old man as some have suggested. He is only 31, and the O's are desperate for someone to hit behind Cal Ripken in the lineup. Cal and the O's are going to have one long year if no one ever has to throw him a strike. As it turns out though, Bob Horner is not the answer. Weeks later he announces his retirement, feeling unsure that he has recovered enough to help the Orioles. So like the decision on the opposite side of the infield, Frank bases his choice on defense. Larry Sheets will stay a DH only. Randy Milligan and Jim Traber will platoon at first.

At second base, Pete Stanicek, who played 83 games for the O's in '88, will take on weak-hitting Billy Ripken. Stanicek is hurt much of spring training however, and loses the job partly by default to Billy. Even had Stanicek stayed healthy, it is a sure bet Robinson would have gone for the better defensive player again, and probably chosen Ripken.

Only the catching position seems to settle early. Mickey Tettleton, the Oakland A's castoff, and Bob Melvin, from the Giants, are both fine defensive catchers who can handle a young pitching staff confidently. The only question is whether Frank will decide to carry a third catcher, Carl Nichols, who could also play third and the outfield. Once Frank sees the potential talent in the outfield though, Carl has no chance.

Phil Bradley will be one of those outfielders. Beyond him, there are Brady Anderson, Butch Davis, Steve Finley, Ken Gerhart, Keith Hughes, Ken Landreaux, Joe Orsulak, Rafel Skeete, and Pete Stanicek. In March, they add Mike Devereaux to the possibilities. The biggest battle develops in centerfield, where Brady Anderson and a non-roster kid named Steve Finley are playing. Both are fast as the wind, full of enthusiasm and desire. They are diving all over the place, crashing into fences, and making spectacular catches all over the field. They appear to be clones of one another. Finley has caught the Orioles completely by surprise. His meteoric rise through the farm system has all occurred in one short year. Was he ready for this? Frank says only one can go back to Baltimore. On opening day though, there's Brady Anderson in center field. Next to him in right is Steve Finley. That, however, is just the beginning. Mike Devereaux proves to be just as fast and agile as the Birds' other two gazelles. He too lands a spot on the roster. The club's best hitter last year, Joe

Orsulak, is obviously going to have to share some playing time. The defense in the outfield becomes the most noticeably improved aspect of the '89 O's. Can they hit? No one knows.

As each spot is filled, the O's first think defense. Even the last utility spot in the infield is won by a non-roster player, Rene Gonzales. A weak hitter, Rene's defense is artistic, and he can play at second, short, or third. Rick Schu, a much better hitter, makes the team only when Bill Ripken must go on the disabled list as spring training ends.

Pitching is also a complete unknown. Midway through the exhibition season, though, there is room for some very quiet optimism. The staff has an ERA of 3.09. They have given up only one home run in 64 innings. The starters begin to fall into place. Dave Schmidt, pitching almost exclusively in relief for the Birds the last two years, will be starter number one. He has earned it, being the only regular with a winning record during the last two horrendous seasons. The remainder of the rotation will be kids: Jose Bautista (24), Bob Milacki (24), Jeff Ballard (25), and Pete Harnisch (22). Frank Robinson knows there is potential here, and the future indeed looks promising. Exactly when "the future" will begin is difficult to say.

The relief staff has more veterans, but also more questions. Brian Holton will make the team as will Mark Thurmond, a much needed left hander, and Mark Williamson. The Marks are returning from last year. The Birds' number one draft pick, Gregg Olson, was pitching last year at this time for the Auburn Tigers. Surely a conservative Oriole organization will send him to AA or AAA this year. But Gregg has an incredible spring, pitching to a 0.00 ERA. There is no way the Birds can send him down.

Of all the great stories in spring training however, Kevin Hickey's becomes the most Cinderella-like. At 33 years of age, Hickey does not fit in the O's rebuilding plans. Not only that, Kevin's last appearance in the major leagues was in 1983. After that an assortment of injuries kept him down in the minors. No less than four major league teams released him, and he played for nine minor league teams in five years. He never gave up though. In '88, the Birds sent him to AA Charlotte, and finally to AAA Rochester. He was so broke he lived in the Oriole clubhouse. He came to spring training as a non-roster player with no chance to make the club. But he keeps firing and keeps firing, striking out left-handed batters one after another. His intensity and drive so impress Frank Robinson that Kevin finds himself in a major league uniform for the first time in six years. There is not a happier person in Memorial Stadium on opening day than Kevin Hickey.

Hickey's drive is symbolic of the entire team the 1989 Orioles are becoming. These guys are excited, not just in making the team, but about their chances in the upcoming season. They actually feel they can win some games. Steve Finley, a guy who by his looks could easily be mistaken for a high school player, expresses the thought of the team. He says that many on the team had been at Rochester last year, not Baltimore. Rochester had won, and he didn't see any reason why they could not continue winning at the major league level.

Of course, no one else does. No one. One after another every sporting publication, television show, and radio show makes their preseason predictions. Each time, the Orioles are chosen to finish last. Last. Dead last. One syndicated radio show hosted by Tony Kubek has a discussion about how difficult it is to choose winners. They therefore decide not to chastise each other for their selections, unless of course, someone would be delirious enough to choose the Orioles. *Sports Illustrated's* Peter Gammons says, "It's a season that may seem to last forever to Cal Ripken, Jr., the Orioles' one and only star." *Sport* magazine's selections are authored by Tim Kurkjian. Tim covers the Orioles on a daily basis for the *Baltimore Sun*, so he, more than anyone knows what the Orioles have. "The Orioles are terrible and they're going to finish in last place again, but you have to credit them for one thing: at least they recognize that." Why they will finish 7th? "Because they stink." Final numbers: "65-97." A local article by Jim Henneman of the *Baltimore Evening Sun* is the closest to being optimistic: "They are headed in the right direction with pitching and defense as the foundation, but 70 wins might be the limit this year." Prediction? Last place.

In desperation it becomes necessary to check the prediction of an admittedly biased prognosticator, someone who is hoping against hope that the Baltimore Orioles will improve, someone who can only be considered a ridiculously over-optimistic fan. That, of course, is me.

The prediction: Orioles - 5th place - 77-85. There. Someone has predicted that the Orioles will not finish last.

THE OPENING DAY ROSTER

Pitchers	Throws	Age	Major League Service
Jeff Ballard	Left	25	1 Year
Jose Bautista	Right	24	1 Year
Pete Harnisch	Right	22	2 Games (Rookie)
Kevin Hickey	Left	33	3 Years (Six years ago)
Brian Holton	Right	29	2¾ Years
Bob Milacki	Right	24	3 Games (Rookie)
Gregg Olson	Right	22	1 Month (Rookie)
Dave Schmidt	Right	31	7½ Years
Mark Thurmond	Left	32	5½ Years
Mark Williamson	Right	29	1¾ Years
Catchers	**Bats-Throws**		
Bob Melvin	R-R	27	3½ Years
Mickey Tettleton	S-R	28	4½ Years
Infielders			
Rene Gonzales	R-R	27	2 Years
Randy Milligan	R-R	27	½ Year
Bill Ripken*	R-R	24	1½ Years
Cal Ripken	R-R	28	7½ Years
Rick Schu	R-R	27	4 Years
Jim Traber	L-L	27	1½ Years
Craig Worthington	R-R	23	1 Month (Rookie)
Outfielders			
Brady Anderson	L-L	25	¾ Year
Phil Bradley	R-R	30	5 Years
Mike Devereaux	R-R	25	¼ Year (Rookie)
Steve Finley	L-L	23	None (Rookie)
Joe Orsulak	L-L	26	4 Years
Designated Hitter			
Larry Sheets	L-R	29	4 Years

On disabled list.

CHAPTER SEVEN

The New Beginning

April 3, 1989, Memorial Stadium, Baltimore, Maryland. There is some doubt the Baltimore Orioles and Boston Red Sox will be able to open the 1989 baseball season today, but as game time approaches, the gray winterlike sky is replaced with sunshine. 52,161 hopeful fans have packed the park. It is difficult to erase the thought of last year's opening day debacle, when the Birds lost 12-0. Oriole fans are also well aware of the fact that President Bush will throw out the first ball. The O's are 0-4 when a president has thrown out the first ball in their park. Who invited him, anyway?

Still, this is the new beginning, a new team, a new attitude. This is also opening day, and you cannot help but feel a tingly electricity run through your body. Brooks Robinson, the color commentator on the local Oriole television coverage confesses that he felt that "high" coming to the park today, a certain "anxiety" and tenseness.

The "new" Frank Robinson is having a closed-door

meeting with his young players. As the meeting breaks, the players are high-spirited, excited, shaking hands with each other and roaring to play. The Birds' public address announcer, Rex Barney, is starting his 20th year with the club. He is announcing the starting lineups, and the anticipation and excitement is building to a fevered pitch. Just hearing his voice makes Oriole fans think of the great baseball they have witnessed here: "...and pitching for the Boston Red Sox, number 21, Roger Clemens...." Rex finishes with two simple words that send more chills up the spines of the fans, "Thank youuuuuuuu," and you know it is time for baseball. The national anthem is sung by Joan Jett, rock star and Oriole fan. Baltimore fans, a patriotic lot, stand quietly during the performance of the song that was written in their hometown. Near the end of the "Banner" however, they interject one extra word into the song, knowing that Francis Scott Key would not mind. "Gave proof through the night that our flag was still there, O's! Oh say, does that star-spangled banner yet wave, O'er the land of the free and the home of the brave!" Cheers ensue, and then it happens. The 1989 Baltimore Orioles take the field. The place erupts.

There is no resemblance between the team on the field and the one that stood there last year at this time. Well one, Cal Ripken remains the same. In their new uniforms with the ornithologically correct birds on the hat, they bear a strong resemblance to an Oriole team of yesteryear. With all those kids out there, you cannot help but think of the 1960 team.

Finally, the first pitch, and the wait is over. The best hitter in baseball, Wade Boggs, grounds to first, and another ovation follows. Rookie Craig Worthington at third displays the youngsters' jitters when he bobbles the next grounder, but he recovers in time to throw out Marty Barrett. The Sox go in order, and the kids sprint off the field in excitement. Roger Clemens, the great one, takes the mound. Dan Shaughnessy, columnist for the *Boston Globe*, has predicted that Roger will no-hit the Birds on the first day of the season. As he retires the first six batters, the fans get a bit uneasy.

In the top of the third however, they get to see their first view of their new Orioles. Rookie Steve Finley races back into right field, making a great catch before crashing full tilt into the fence. His efforts would cost him a shoulder separation and an immediate visit to the disabled list. But the tone was set. In the fourth, the O's are at it again. Marty Barrett attempts to sacrifice bunt Boggs to second, but Mickey Tettleton pounces on a good bunt and throws out Boggs. Mike Greenwell then hits a blast in the left center power alley, but Brady Anderson makes a great running catch to keep the game scoreless.

In the bottom of the fourth, the Birds display their new brand of offense. Brady Anderson walks, and then steals second base. Joe Orsulak, in for Steve Finley, singles him home with a base hit up the middle. The fans are ecstatic as their Orioles take the lead.

In the sixth, Dave Schmidt, pitching a masterful game, begins to tire. Boggs doubles; Evans doubles; and Greenwell connects for a home run and a 3-1 Sox lead. The crowd stirs again, and you can almost hear their unified thought, "Here we go again." This however, is a new year. In the bottom of the inning, Brady Anderson doubles, and newcomer Phil Bradley walks behind him. Joe Orsulak shows that the O's did learn a thing or two in spring training. He hits behind the runners, advancing them to second and third. Here comes Cal Ripken, and the situation everyone has talked about has developed in the first game. Cal Ripken is up with one out, first base open, and no Eddie Murray in the on-deck circle. Clemens pitches carefully to Cal, but does not walk him. He fouls off Roger's toughest stuff, and then deposits a 2-2 pitch over the left field fence. The Birds go up 4-3, and the crowd is delirious.

In the seventh, the Sox get to Schmidt again, who is obviously out of gas. Kevin Hickey, the Orioles' oldest player at 33, comes in for the sole purpose of getting out Wade Boggs, which he does. Brian Holton, the old Dodger, is Robinson's next pitcher. Craig Worthington makes another great play going to his left, stopping the BoSox threat and stopping the big inning. It's tied 4-4.

In the ninth, the Sox are ready to win it. Nick Esasky booms a shot off the left field wall, but Phil Bradley plays the carom perfectly and throws a strike to second, holding Esasky to a single. Oriole fans cannot believe what they are seeing. On the next pitch, Boston tries a hit and run. Jody Reed swings and misses and Tettleton guns down Esasky. For the fifth time on opening day the Oriole defense has saved the game.

Extra innings. Another defensive gem in center in the tenth as Brady holds Boggs at second on a long drive. That takes the O's into the bottom of the 11th, where Randy Milligan comes up with his second hit in a row after batting for Traber against the left-handed throws of Rob Murphy. Tettleton goes to third on the hit. That brings up the rookie Craig Worthington with one out. In the bottom of the ninth Worthington came up in the exact same situation, but was unsuccessful. This time the BoSox change pitchers, and move Mike Greenwell in to play five infielders and two outfielders. Frank Robinson pulls Craig aside for a few words of encouragement and an opportunity to calm his nerves. Worthington walks up, slices one into left field, and the Birds win 5-4. A mass of Orioles meet at home plate, slapping and hugging. No, it's not the World Series, but baseball is fun again in Baltimore.

O's fans are chomping at the bit after the Birds are rained out on April 5. So on Thursday the 6th, 22,000 fans show up to see 24-year-old Jose Bautista and his forkball. It is the largest home crowd for a second game in Baltimore since 1955. The O's fall behind early 3-0, but come back with their new style of offense. Brady Anderson steals third; Sheets singles. It's 3-2. Rene Gonzales doubles; Anderson bunts him over to third. Worthington singles him home. In the seventh, Tettleton socks a home run, and the Birds win again 6-4. Appreciative O's fans give Tettleton a standing ovation. But they do the same thing in the fourth and fifth innings when runners are bunted up from second to third. Home runs are nice, but having an Oriole team that can bunt and sacrifice? That would win ball games.

Once again, the defense takes the pressure off Bautista by making stellar plays behind him, the most spectacular of which is Brady Anderson's diving catch off the bat of Jody Reed. It is the second game of the season, and the Birds have already won more games than they did all of last April.

Next, the Birds hit the road on a 10-game trip. In '88, they had gone 3-16 on this trip. They open in Minnesota, where rookie Bob Milacki shuts out the power laden Twins for five innings. But in the sixth he comes unglued, and the Birds lose 8-3. In game two, Dave Schmidt, the opening day starter, has nothing. A five-run second inning is wasted, and the Birds lose 6-5. Sunday, April 9 in the Metrodome young Jeff Ballard, a lifetime 10-20 pitcher with a 5.09 ERA in two partial seasons with the O's gets his first start of the year. As luck would have it, he gets to face Cy Young winner, Frank Viola, who is only 23-2 in the Metrodome, and 3-0 versus the O's last season. But like opening day, these young Birds do not care when they are supposed to lose. Ballard pitches a gem, giving up only a solo home run to Kent Hrbek, and becomes the first visiting left-hander to go the distance in the Homerdome since September of 1987. The offense roughs up Viola, including a three-run home run by Randy Milligan and a two-run shot by Cal. O's win 8-1.

The horror of last season follows the Birds everywhere, but no where worse than their next stop, Kansas City. In 1988, the Birds lost all twelve games to K.C. Game one this year proves to be no different. Bret Saberhagen pitches a three-hit shutout, and the O's youngest starter, Pete Harnisch, victimizes himself with a balk in the sixth inning, which sets up two of K.C.'s three runs. The next day the Royals make it 15 in a row. They win 6-5 when the O's give up three home runs, deliver two wild pitches, and leave two men in scoring position. Now this looks more like a rookie team is supposed to look. The only question seems to be, can K.C. do to the Orioles what the Birds did to them in 1969 and 1970, namely win 23 straight games? The answer comes the next day, but only after 15 innings. Bob Milacki pitches 6 1/3 innings, giving up just one run. The Birds score three in the fifth with two bunts and an infield hit. In the eighth, Craig Worthington, quickly becoming a clutch-hitter for the O's, singles through a drawn-up infield to make it 4-1. But the Royals score three in the ninth, and the battle continues into the 15th inning. Gregg Olson, the last pitcher in the bullpen, gets two ground-outs in the 15th with George Brett at second base to hold the Royals. In the bottom of the inning, the O's manufacture the winning run. Orsulak singles to right, steals second on a pitchout, goes to third on a deep fly ball to right, and scores on rookie Mike Devereaux's sacrifice fly to medium left. The Birds win 5-4. Taking advantage of every opportunity, they get the K.C. monkey off their back, and get back to .500. How could the O's win a game like this when they couldn't in '88? Frank gives his thoughts. "They thought they were going to win, and that's the difference on this team. A guy would come out of the game, and instead of coming in here (the locker room to escape the cold), he'd stay in the dugout and cheer for his teammates. That shows me something."

This, of course, is also a completely different Oriole team. In their first seven games they have made only two errors. More importantly, they are catching balls they never reached in the last few years. They are leading the league at this early juncture in fielding and sacrifice bunts.

In Boston, where the O's have lost 12 of their last 13, they win one of the three, pounding the Red Sox 12-4 on Saturday. Oriole fans are ecstatic. It has been a very long time since the Orioles beat up on anyone, much less an AL East team in their own ballpark. In addition, no one in the AL East is running away from the pack. After Saturday's game the O's find themselves at 5-5, tied for first place. Yes, first place. O's fans are running for their newspapers, and just staring at the standings. Never mind that no one in the division is overpowering. Of course, it is still April, BUT THE ORIOLES ARE IN FIRST PLACE! Jim Traber says, "You can't really say we're going to contend, but for 10 games we have. I honestly think we can finish in the top four. That's not a prediction. But it's not crazy either. I think it's reality."

Rene Gonzales adds, "Everyone in here is excited. You

73

can sense something different.''

With another rainout on Sunday, the Birds have more time to consider what is happening here. Their team has a grand total of four errors, the same total that Eddie Murray alone has playing with the L.A. Dodgers. They are the only team in the major leagues that has not allowed an unearned run. They have led in nine of their 10 games, they have come from behind in three of their five wins. Larry Sheets adds, ''We may still finish last, but I guarantee you we've changed some people's opinions of the Baltimore Orioles. It's not a fluke when we win. It's not a fluke when we go into a place and win a series.... Now we've got guys that want to go out and get dirty. If they're not in the lineup, they get upset. We're young, and we're going to make mistakes, but we're going to improve too. Right now we're 5-5 and everyone says it's a surprise. We could very easily be 8-2. We've been in every game except one.''

The Birds are coming home to play their nemesis again, the K.C. Royals. Billy Ripken is also coming off the disabled list. In game one, the game goes 13 innings, but the O's lose it 7-4. They come back to win game two 6-5. In the series finale, it is Bret Saberhagen again, this time versus Jeff Ballard. But once again, the O's break the odds, and Ballard does it again. He goes 8 1/3 innings, allowing only two runners to reach scoring position. The Birds squeeze across two runs, and Mark Williamson comes on to get the final two Royals. A 2-0 shutout and Jeff Ballard becomes the first Oriole pitcher in 16 years to win his first three games. His ERA is now a neat 1.17.

George Brett wants to know who this Jeff Ballard person is. ''This guy's not the same pitcher. Last year he had a straight fastball, a curve, and a change. Now he's got two breaking balls, a change-up that's a screw ball, and a fastball that moves."

Ballard says, "My stuff isn't close to most of the pitchers up here." So in the winter, he worked his butt off. He also studied with his mentor, Dave McNally, the O's crafty left-hander of another era. In 1988, he was one of Mike Boddicker's favorite students. Then, before the season started, new pitching coach Al Jackson added a subtle change to his delivery that kept everything down in the strike zone. Ballard looks very hittable like McNally and Boddicker, but now he's getting more people out and never hurting himself. All of this is brand new for Ballard. "I've *never* been involved in a 1-0 or 2-0 game before. This was new territory. I'll say this; we've been battling. We play great defense and we get some key hits. It's a heck of a lot of fun right now."

When it is over, the O's have taken a series from the Royals for the first time since July of 1987.

Next up are the Twins in Baltimore. The O's take two of three, winning the last game 3-0 on a Bob Milacki three-hitter. He faces the minimum 27 batters against a Twins team that has been scoring big versus everyone. The defense turns four double plays behind him, and Tettleton throws out the other attempting to steal, eliminating every base runner. It is the Birds' second shutout in four days. Milacki has allowed only one run in his last 16 innings. Two of the three Oriole runs once again are scored on hustle. Brady Anderson tries to score from third on a grounder to second. The ball beats him home, but he knocks it out of Laudner's glove to score. In the meantime, speedy Mike Devereaux goes all the way to third, later scoring on a Cal Ripken double.

The bad news is that Bob Melvin, the Orioles' leading

hitter at .345, fractures his right index finger. He will be replaced by catcher Chris Hoiles from Rochester. The good news is that Steve Finley will be returning after his run-in with the fence on opening day.

April 24 is the beginning of a seven-day, West Coast road trip. The O's split with California when they lose the opener 3-2, blowing six chances to score a runner from second base. But in game two, Jeff Ballard does it again. He scatters six hits over seven innings, leaving the game with a groin pull the O's hope against hope is not serious. Frank Robinson looks like a miracle man choosing a lineup with five players hitting under .210. They come through with four home runs, clubbing California 8-1. Every time Ballard has taken the mound he has come through with an important victory, and the hitters seem to always come through with an outburst of runs.

Next stop is Oakland, and the AL champion A's. Can the Birds compete with the big boys? Game one proves to be another pitching battle with Bob Welch and Jose Bautista. Welch takes a 1-0 lead into the eighth inning, pitching a one-hitter. But then Frank makes all the right moves. After a Jim Traber walk, he pinch hits Joe Orsulak for Worthington. Orsulak also works Welch for a walk. Milligan comes in to run for Traber. Billy Ripken then attempts a sacrifice bunt, but pops it up. It falls between the onlooking Mark McGwire and Ron Hassey. Frank then pinch hits for Brady Anderson for the first time this year, with Mike Devereaux. Mike proceeds to work relief pitcher Greg Cadaret for a walk and a 1-1 tie. Then Steve Finley comes through with a base hit to score the go-ahead run.

Next Frank moves Finley from right to center field, just in time for Steve to make a diving catch off the bat of Walt

Weiss. To top it off, he brings in Gregg Olson in his first real role as a closer. Olson retires six A's in a row (with help from Finley), including striking out the side in the ninth against the likes of Dave Parker, Dave Henderson, and Mark McGwire, the heart of the A's potent lineup. His incredible curve ball actually buckles the knees of the threesome. It is the kind of game Oriole fans only dreamed about in the last few years, the kind of game that makes them think that maybe, just maybe, ORIOLES MAGIC has returned.

Reality returns, however, as Pete Harnisch struggles terribly in his first game back after 16 days with the flu. After the 9-4 loss, Harnisch will return to Rochester, to be replaced by Jay Tibbs, who has gone 3-0 with a 0.93 ERA down on the farm. The O's go on to lose two more.

On Saturday the 29th in Seattle, Frank is giving his team a lecture about not getting careless. Things are slipping. There was a botched rundown in Oakland, a misplayed ball off the wall in Anaheim, and then Tettleton didn't get up immediately after he dived for a wild throw in Seattle. That allowed the winning run to score. The O's are not playing the same defense they had earlier in the month. The lecture is followed by a rare Billy Ripken error on Sunday, allowing Seattle to score the first run. It is the third unearned run in three games, after allowing just one in the first 21. But then, everything turns around. Jeff Ballard, the new loss-streak ender, does it again. He keeps things close, losing 3-2 going into the eighth. The O's have once again scored their two runs on a sacrifice fly and two bunts. Then in the eighth, Mickey Tettleton comes through with a huge, two-run home run and a come-from-behind 4-3 victory. It breaks the three game skein, and makes Jeff Ballard 5-0 for the month of April.

"Other than opening day," Frank Robinson says, "This was probably our biggest game of the year. This was the first time we had what you would call a down situation. We had a chance to lose four in a row, then go home and have a day off to think about it." But the Birds came through, ending the month at 12-12, in a first place tie with the New York Yankees.

Jeff Ballard is named AL pitcher of the month with a 5-0 record and a 1.46 ERA. In the long line of great Oriole pitchers, it is the best April a Bird has ever had.

CHAPTER EIGHT

It's Early, But...

It is May, and all of baseball is ready for the Oriole collapse. They have survived the first month of the season, when weird things often happen. They are playing in a division where no one has taken charge. In May, though, things will return to normal and surely the inevitable will occur: the Birds will return to the basement where they belong. Right?

On May 2, the inevitable is delayed when the Birds win the first contest of the month 4-3 at home versus the Angels. The O's bats have gone silent, but they take advantage of 10 California walks, squeezing across two in the seventh and one in the ninth. Jose Bautista, who would now like to be called J.J., has made his third quality start in four outings, giving up six hits in seven innings. Gregg Olson comes in to shut down the Angels in both the eighth and ninth, retiring six of seven batters. A collective sigh of relief is heard from the O's dugout, seeing that Olson seems unaffected after getting hit by a line drive in Seattle.

"Nothing seems to bother this team," says Frank Robinson. "They scrap and scrap and if the other team isn't careful, we'll win the game. You have to credit the pitchers because they seem to know if they hold the other team down, we'll have a chance to win. You have to give the hitters credit because they didn't get discouraged."

The offense however, has gone dormant. Bob Milacki, who is quickly becoming known as the Birds' hard-luck pitcher, must suffer the brunt of the dead offense immediately. He matches up Thursday night against Bert Blylevan in a titanic pitching struggle. Blylevan allows six hits and seven walks. Still, the Birds cannot score a single tally for Milacki. They go 0-10 with runners in scoring position. In the bottom of the eighth, they load the bases with no outs. Cal Ripken proceeds to strike out and Larry Sheets knocks into a double play. In the ninth, Jack Howell hits a two-run dinger, and the Angels win it 2-0. No longer is anyone questioning that the Birds have improved dramatically in defense and pitching. Sometimes, though, it is proving very difficult for Oriole fans to handle the total lack of offense, especially when the team cannot even manufacture runs.

Rain gives the offense a reprieve on Friday night, May 5th, but it does little good. Seattle proceeds to take both ends of a doubleheader on Saturday night, 2-1 and 6-5. In the first game, the Birds leave another seven on base and have now failed to plate a run in scoring position 21 straight times. Game two produces more offense, explainable only because Jeff Ballard is on the mound. But this time it's not enough as Ballard gets bombed for 5 runs in 1 2/3 innings. On Sunday, Seattle completes the sweep, winning 5-3.

Frank jumbles the lineup, moving Cal from cleanup to third, Finley from third to sixth, Orsulak to cleanup, and

Larry Sheets to the bench. The results, however, are the same. Sheets is hitting .204, Traber .206, Worthington .191, and Tettleton .198. Baseball prognosticators shake their collective heads, seeing these numbers, and preparing their "I told you so" speeches. The Birds are pressing, and things are getting worse. They have lost four in a row, seven of their last nine. They are at the lowest point of the season, three games under .500. To make matters worse, guess who is coming to town? The AL Champion Oakland A's, of course.

Those close to the Orioles over the last two years are not panicking, however. They know that the last seven Oriole games have been decided by a grand total of four runs. No one is hitting, but still the Birds are staying close in nearly every game. The outstanding defense is allowing this team to win games even when the bats are slumping. In addition, Bob Melvin, the Orioles' best hitter before his injury, is being reactivated.

The trend, though, continues against Oakland. The Birds lose 6-1, managing just four hits. The predicted demise of the Birds is in full swing. Newspapers around the country forecast the complete collapse of the O's in the next two weeks. The fun stuff is over.

On May 9, the Orioles are on the verge of their sixth straight loss. The A's are up 3-0 after 4 1/2 innings. The Birds' offense is dead. Then an event occurs that causes Oriole fans to sit back and wonder if there is an outside influence affecting their team. With three outs to go before an official game, umpire Don Denkinger decides it is raining too hard to continue. Play is stopped. Manager Tony LaRussa cannot believe it. Surely they can play another 1/2 inning. Denkinger says no. It continues to rain all night and

81

continues through the next night. The bullet has missed the Orioles' heart.

The A's hang around town to play a rare weekday afternoon game on Thursday. With the last-minute decision to play, much of Baltimore does not find out that the game has been rescheduled until too late. Only 1201 people show up at the park, the third lowest crowd in Oriole history. Before an empty stadium the undefeated Dave Stewart will face 5-1 Jeff Ballard. Stewart is the hottest pitcher in baseball at this young stage of the season. The Orioles do not care. Their anemic offense unloads its frustrations on Stewart with 12 hits, the most given up by Dave in his entire career. Ballard comes through with what has become his average performance, 7 innings, 9 hits, 0 walks, and 1 run.

On the verge of going under, the Birds turn a near certain 3-0 loss two nights ago into a 6-2 win against the League's best pitcher. In fact, the O's are now 7-2 versus pitchers with previous 20-win seasons. In a season of critical wins, this could be one of the biggest.

The next night, with the White Sox in town, Bob Melvin returns to spark the offense, and the Birds explode for 9 runs. Cal Ripken is knocking the cover off the ball since Frank has moved him to third in the lineup. But the O's cannot stop the ChiSox from scoring. Enter the Cinderella kid, Kevin Hickey, to face his former team. He goes 2 1/3 innings, stopping the White Sox cold, and recording his first save of the year. At 33, Kevin Hickey is the oldest Oriole, but when he gets that last out he leaps into the air with the excitement you would expect from a little-league pitcher. On a team of enthusiastic players, Hickey may just be the most exuberant.

But now that the hitting has returned, it seems the starting pitching is collapsing. The O's lose the next two with Chicago as Bob Milacki and J.J. Bautista both get shelled.

The Orioles have now lost 10 of their last 14 games. In the last seven, the opponents have totaled 10 or more hits in each game. The ERA has ballooned from 3.97 to 4.35. To top things off, the O's new ace, Jeff Ballard, has a groin pull and will miss at least his next start. There is particular concern about Bautista, the guy many expected to carry this young team. Even his manager cannot distinguish his forkball from his fastball. His velocity is down. He looks tentative.

The Birds travel to Texas, and Dave Schmidt comes through with a masterful performance just in the nick of time. He pitches a 5-hitter over seven innings, and the O's hitting continues. Mickey Tettleton has come out of nowhere. He cracks his eighth home run of the season, and no one can figure where the sudden power surge has come from. Tonight, though, everyone in the lineup gets a hit, and the Birds roll 8-2. It is the first win by a starter other than Ballard since April 26.

No one in the AL East has taken control as the Birds return home to play Cleveland. Boston, New York, and the Indians are all hovering around .500, allowing the Birds to stay close to the pack. No one is thinking about that, though. Frank Robinson just wants his young pitchers to keep progressing, and to continue to see his team play good, solid baseball.

On Thursday night, the 18th, they do just that. "Hard luck" Milacki has once again drawn the opponent's ace, this time Greg Swindell. They battle pitch for pitch, but Milacki finds himself down 2-0 in the sixth. Finally, in the bottom of the inning, the Birds break through and score against

Swindell for the first time in 28 2/3 innings at Memorial Stadium. Phil Bradley races to his sixth triple of the young season. This is the most triples hit by an Oriole during an entire year since 1984. Cal comes up and singles him home. Then in the seventh, rookie Mike Devereaux, getting into the lineup more and more often, makes things happen again. He strokes a single down the first-base line. He steals second. He steals third. Billy Ripken comes through in the clutch, delivering a two-out double, and the game is tied. On to the 10th, when Milacki must finally be lifted. Mark Williamson sets down Cleveland's big boys. Then the Orioles' "do-all-the-little-things-right" offense comes through again. Brady Anderson leads off with a walk and steals second on the first pitch. Bradley hits behind the runner, stroking a shot to right field allowing Brady to move to third. Cal Ripken gets the expected intentional walk, but catcher Bob Melvin comes through with a big single to win it 3-2.

The O's are back to the style of baseball that has quickly become 1989 Oriole baseball. But what impresses everyone is that even when they lose, these Orioles nearly always keep themselves in a position where they have a chance to win. They are playing smart baseball, a brand you might expect from a veteran team. O's fans are impressed and the excitement level in Baltimore is building with each passing day. Once again, the morning conversations at offices all over town are about the Birds. Life is fun again, and 1988, while not forgotten, just makes 1989 that much more inconceivable. This is not supposed to be happening; it is impossible really, and of course it will end. No one is sitting around dreading the inevitable, though. The fans, like the players, are just taking one game at a time, and enjoying them all.

On Friday the 19th, J.J. Bautista returns and gives up two, 2-run dingers and the Birds lose 4-1. Bautista has now given up 11 home runs in 52 2/3 innings. No other AL pitcher has allowed more than seven. Pitching coach Al Jackson is not a happy camper. Oriole pitchers are to do three things: throw strikes, make the batter hit the ball, and keep the ball in the park so the great defense can haul it down. J.J. is failing miserably with item three. Frank sends him to the bullpen to work out his problems. Brian Holton and Jay Tibbs move in as starters as the O's return to a five man rotation. Robinson looks at the move as a temporary one, hoping the kids like Harnisch and Bautista will be back soon. For now, though, there is little choice.

Holton pitches well in his first outing, going six innings, the longest stint of his career. But the O's lose 2-0, and the recent inconsistency continues as the Birds win one and lose one, win one....

They embark on a six-game road trip to Chicago and Cleveland. They leave with a record of 18-21. This trip will most likely determine how much longer the Birds will remain competitive in the division race.

They open with a bang. Dave Schmidt takes a perfect game into the sixth inning. Mike Devereaux, now another cog in what has already become the best defensive outfield in baseball, nearly hits for the cycle. Schmidt settles for a combined three-hitter, as Robinson continues to groom his relief pitchers for the roles he sees them filling. Kevin Hickey goes an inning as set-up man, the guy who is sent in to get out left-handers. Gregg Olson, with only a few months of major league experience, is Robinson's choice for closer. Tonight he works a nonpressure ninth inning gaining more experience. The incredible defense continues. The highlight of this

85

game is provided by left fielder Phil Bradley who makes a diving, sprawling catch off the bat of Dan Pasqua. The O's win 5-1, and they have fun doing it.

The fun continues the next night as the O's finally score some runs for Bob Milacki, who had pitched into the ninth inning on three previous occasions without getting a victory. This night he wins 9-3. But the big surprise comes in the last game of the series. Jay Tibbs makes his first start for the Birds. At this point in the season it has become obvious that comparisons with last year's Oriole team are ludicrous. But this guy Tibbs did pitch for the '88 Birds. In fact, he set a club record losing his last 10 decisions in a row. His ERA was a ridiculous 5.39. He was, in a word, terrible. No wonder Frank Robinson said this would be a temporary move. But Tibbs goes out and pitches six eye-popping innings of shutout ball. The Birds win again 8-0. Just like the team itself, Jay Tibbs bears no resemblance to the pitcher of last year. What is happening here? How can this be explained? Has Tibbs added some new mysterious pitch to his repertoire? Well, no, in fact Tibbs says all he has done is junk a pitch. He no longer is throwing his curve. Oriole fans begin to wonder about the mystical qualities of their team.

The win takes the Birds back to .500 for the first time in three weeks. The sweep of the series is the first three-game streak of their season, and their first sweep on the road since August of 1987. Over the last eight games, the team ERA is 1.60, their best stretch since 1982. Thinking that these raw kids have performed better than the 1983 world championship club even for a very short period of time is baffling. There are few explanations, only more results.

Cleveland is the next victim. On May 26 the Birds take their fourth in a row, and go into sole possession of first place. Jeff Ballard and Gregg Olson do it again. They combine for a seven-hitter and win 5-2 on a night when neither said they felt particularly good. Once again the backbone of the performance is the defense. First Brady Anderson runs down a rocket into left center off the bat of Oddibe McDowell. Then in the fourth inning, with runners on first and third and one out, Cal and Billy turn a shot that Ballard thinks is a double into an inning ending double play. It is the O's seventh win in nine games.

"This club has a calm confidence," Robinson says. "This is one more game in the win column and that's how the players feel. We want to enjoy it, then focus on the next one. It's a good feeling but we just go out and play. We'll have some bad stretches and we'll keep the same attitude. These guys are professionals in every sense of the word."

It is May 27, and the win streak goes to five. Schmidt pitches well again, but Robinson pulls him after five innings. Frank's strategy of going early and often to the bullpen is paying off with big dividends. The O's win 5-1, and a funny thing is happening to Mickey Tettleton. He is being walked more and more, twice in this contest, yet he still hits home run number 11, matching his highest season output ever. It is his two-run shot in the eighth that puts this game away. Suddenly, no one wants to know who will hit behind Cal Ripken, or how Cal will ever get anything to hit.

The streak ends the next day as Greg Swindell faces Bob "hard luck" Milacki. Milacki gives up two hits over eight sterling innings, taking a 0-0 game into the ninth. The O's lose when Joe Carter bunts home Felix Fermin off Mark Williamson. The O's are playing their best ball of the year, however, and they are now coming home to close out the month against the Rangers.

87

They are greeted by 32,263 berserk fans as they take the field to take on the bionic arm of Nolan Ryan. The fireballing Ryan is facing the junk ball throws of Brian Holton, another game that appears to be a huge mismatch. But the Birds blast three 'taters off Ryan, the first time that has happened to Nolan in nearly seven years. Tettleton hits number 12, putting him in a tie for the league lead. Robinson's pitching by committee method works again, as Holton combines with three relief pitchers to pitch a six-hitter and win 6-1. Not only has the relief pitching been incredible, but the defense continues to play near perfect baseball. Robinson looks like a wizard, inserting a new pitcher at just the right time. Now, on top of all this incredible play, Memorial Stadium is being visited again by someone Oriole fans never expected to see, at least this year. It is The Doctor—Doctor Longball.

On Tuesday and Wednesday, there is more of the same. Jay Tibbs comes back with another unbelievable performance, followed by Mark Thurmond, Mark Williamson, and Gregg Olson. Bird relief pitchers are shutting down everyone. Phil Bradley takes charge offensively in the Orioles' "new-hero-every-night" program, and the O's win 6-2. On Wednesday, things are going great guns again. Jeff Ballard is winning 4-0 in the fifth when Pete Incaviglia hits a vicious line drive up the middle. Ballard is struck flush in the neck. He leaves the game, but amazingly appears to be okay. The Rangers rough up replacement Mark Huismann to take the lead 5-4. But the O's are playing on another plateau now. They come right back in the bottom of the sixth, Billy Ripken doubles; Brady Anderson doubles him home; Phil Bradley walks, and then it happens again. Mickey Tettleton blasts another three-run homer, his 13th of the year.

Williamson and Olson shut the door again, and the Birds win a thriller 8-5.

Oriole fans are in a frenzy. After the Tettleton shot, the fans want a curtain call, and they won't stop yelling until Tettleton appears. "The players kind of pushed me out," Tettleton says. "I didn't know what to think. My heart was just pounding." It is the first curtain call of Tettleton's career.

Earlier in the week, Oriole broadcaster Tom Davis was interviewing Mickey's wife Sylvia, in the stands. She revealed that Mickey's new-found home run power might be attributed to his breakfast cereal. No, not the "Breakfast of Champions," but instead, Froot Loops. Within the week the sugar-coated O's were not to be found in Baltimore area grocery stores. Fans were taking them to the game and tossing them like confetti. Kids pleaded with their moms to let them eat Froot Loops like Mickey. The players were thinking of changing Tettleton's already new nickname of "The Mick" to "Babe Loops." Yes, this is Mickey Tettleton, the guy released by the Oakland A's, leading the league in home runs at this stage of the season. Tettleton says he's going to clip the "league leaders" from the newspaper for his scrapbook to prove it happened.

All of this is too much to handle. The O's end May at 26-22, the first AL East team to be four games over .500. They have won 11 of their last 14. They have beaten the likes of Nolan Ryan, Dave Stewart, Bret Saberhagen, Frank Viola, and Roger Clemens. Their defense is far and away the best in baseball. Their manager knows exactly when to pull every pitcher and has kept his young players positive all year. They resurrect a pitcher with 10 previous straight losses who is now throwing to a 1.69 ERA. They are stealing bases, hitting behind runners, sacrificing, manufacturing runs. Now, their journeyman catcher is leading the league in home runs. This is heady stuff, fantasy stuff. A look at the record book shows that only one team in the history of baseball has gone from last place to first in one year, and that was 100 years ago. Then when you consider that the '88 Birds were not just in last place, but one of the worst teams ever, well, this is just too much.

The players and coaches, though, are not thinking about such things. They are just having fun, playing well, and by the way, winning. After all, it is only May.

CHAPTER NINE

The Long Wait for the June Swoon

In the early spring of 1989, just before the baseball season was about to begin, a group of co-workers were sitting around after an exceptionally difficult day on the job. In their attempts to commiserate with each other, they resorted to a game of listing the most difficult jobs in the country. One would say, "Well, it could be worse, we could be marketing saccharin."

Another would say, "Yeah, we could be selling Yugos."

The third response brought a quick halt to the "Can-you-top-this?" game. "Well, it could be worse, we could be the marketing and promotion staff for the Baltimore Orioles."

Three months later the real promotion staff for the O's looks just as brilliant as everyone else associated with the club. Their advertising slogan for the 1989 Orioles is plastered all over Baltimore. Frank Robinson is on television repeating the phrase. "THESE ARE EXCITING TIMES.... YOU GOTTA BE THERE." Of course, what they meant was with all the youngsters, the Birds may not win, but at

91

least they would play an exciting brand of baseball, and be exciting to watch develop. But now, people are walking around town saying, "THESE REALLY ARE EXCITING TIMES." Of course, you had to be there, and by golly, no Oriole fan was going to miss this.

As the month begins, though, fans will have to settle for watching their new heroes on television, first in Detroit, then the "Big Apple." The O's are hurting physically. Craig Worthington is out with a pulled hamstring. Randy Milligan is nursing a sore right hand after being hit by a pitch the same night that Ballard was struck in the throat. The bullpen is dog-tired, badly in need of rest. Jim Traber is inserted at first for Milligan. He has had little opportunity to contribute since Milligan won the firstbase position 11 days ago. Randy has played flawless defense and has begun really stinging the ball. Rene Gonzales, the great glove man, gets a chance to play third. In the first inning of the opening game, both subs come to bat. All Traber can manage is a three-run home run. Rene's turn. He, too, homers. And so it goes. No stars, only heroes—new heroes every night. Dave Schmidt is pitching. He is flat, has nothing. He somehow struggles his way through five innings, not allowing the Tigers to break through. Frank then goes to one of only two relievers possibly rested enough to pitch. Mark Thurmond retires 12 of the next 13 Tigers to record his first save, and the Birds do it again 8-3.

The next night Bob Milacki gives the O's a double bonus. He pitches 8 1/3 innings of two-hit ball, both stopping the Tigers and giving the bullpen a rest. Larry Sheets delivers his seventh RBI in as many games. Cal and Billy deliver two hits apiece as do Joe Orsulak and sub Rene Gonzales. It's a 4-1 victory and five in a row.

Saturday night's contest is a nail-biter. With no score in the fifth, Cal Ripken comes up and blasts a two-run shot, only his fourth home run of the year, but second in a week. Brian Holton comes back after a sixth-inning rain delay and can get no one out. Detroit ties it up, 2-2. Tonight, Kevin Hickey is the big gun out of the bullpen, shutting down the Tigers in the seventh and eighth. Jim Traber, still playing for the injured Milligan, comes through again with the go-ahead run. Joe Orsulak goes 3 for 4 and scores another. Gregg Olson takes care of the Tigers in the ninth, and the magic continues, 4-2. Hickey gets his first win, Olson his fifth save, and the Birds have six in a row. They are now on their best stretch since the '83 championship season. They have won 14 of their last 17 and have taken a 4-game lead in the AL East. "Don't say anything about a pennant race," Robinson says. "Wash your mouth out with soap. It's too early for that. We just go out and try to win the game we're playing that day. We're in a stretch where whoever I put out there does the job. Good teams get performances like this."

Yes they do, which is exactly why "THESE ARE EX-CITING TIMES." Bird fans know the Orioles will have some bad stretches, but they also know this team is winning, even when they are not on top of their game. This is a competitive team, and these definitely are "EXCITING TIMES."

Randy Milligan returns to the lineup on Sunday. Not to be outdone, he slugs a three-run homer of his own in the first inning. Phil Bradley adds another blast; Cal goes 3 for 5; Mike Devereaux adds two more, and the Birds do it again, 7-4. Jay Tibbs gives up only one run, but leaves after five innings. The Birds have won seven in a row, but have now gone 35 games without a complete-game victory. Everyone who is anyone in baseball circles says it cannot last. "The staff will burn up in a pennant race."

"By August they will fade into oblivion."

"There's no experience there, and little talent. They will be gone by the All-Star break." Maybe so, but the staff ERA over the last 18 games is 1.93, and Robinson's shuttling of pitchers has been nothing short of genius.

Oriole fans are unconcerned. Their team has won seven in a row, and they are enjoying themselves silly. On to New York and the Birds' first shot at the team Baltimoreans love to hate, the Yankees. In game one, Jeff Ballard takes the mound, and the fans in Baltimore are delirious with glee. The rival Yankees make *six* errors, and the O's pound them into submission. Steve Finley smacks his first grand slam home run, and that is just the beginning. When the smoke clears, it is 16-3. The team that is supposed to be coming apart at the seams has won eight in a row, 16 of their last 19. They are 31-22, five games up on the division. No one is attempting to explain the Orioles' success anymore. The season has become a fairy tale, and fairy tales are not explained with logic.

The streak finally comes to an end on D-day, June 6. Dave LaPoint shuts out the Birds 4-0. Cal Ripken's 11-game hit streak and Joe Orsulak's seven-gamer end also.

After rain stops the Bird attack in the last game of the Yankee series, they return home and back to earth. Milwaukee takes three of four. The lone win comes Friday night when "THE MICK" blasts not one, but two dingers in a 7-1 triumph. Mickey's parents are visiting from Oklahoma to see their son for the first time in Memorial Stadium. Oriole fans suggest they move to Baltimore and attend every game. In the same game, Craig Worthington adds a two-run

94

homer, and Mike Devereaux goes 2 for 4 in his first start against a right-handed pitcher. The losses in the series are not, in themselves, terrible. What really is concerning everyone is Jeff Ballard. He pitches on Saturday night, going into the game number one in the AL in winning percentage (9-1), number two in wins, and number three in ERA (2.12). But after he is bombed for four runs on six hits and three uncharacteristic walks, thoughts cannot help but go back to the line drive he took in the throat. Has his delivery or psyche been affected? To make matters worse, Mark Huismann, who has given the O's some valuable innings out of the pen, leaves the game with a strained right shoulder. With the relievers putting in some massive innings already, Huismann must be put on the 15-day disabled list immediately. They call up J.J. Bautista again.

On Sunday, Jay Tibbs pitches another fine game, but the Birds lose 3-1. B.J. Surhoff steals both second and third off Gregg Olson to set up the winning run. It is a pattern that has developed throughout the series, and Frank Robinson is not happy about it. "All the stolen bases were off the pitchers, and we told them before the series that they ran and ran." The Brewers went 8 for 8 in attempted steals. So instead of enjoying a day off on Monday, Frank schedules an 11:00 A.M. workout at the stadium.

On Tuesday, the dreaded Yankees come to town, and the O's return to the style of baseball they have been playing most of the year. "I think (the workout) helped," says Randy Milligan. "We had been getting a little bit ahead of ourselves, and I think we were a little bit lax during the Milwaukee series." The offense puts together a 13-hit attack, and Dave Schmidt and the unbelievable bullpen combine again for a 5-2 win. "I don't think the workout had anything to do with it," says Robinson. "This club has been able to bounce back all year. When things have gotten tough, they've been able to suck it up and go out and win."

The next night, however, will really test the mettle of this young team that has bounced back so many times already. Bob Milacki is on the mound. He is pitching a superb game. The Ripken boys make it 1-0 in the sixth when Cal singles Billy home. Milacki takes a 1-0 lead into the eighth. But during the game a fog has rolled into Memorial Stadium. It gets progressively worse through the latter innings. In the eighth, Joe Orsulak loses a fly ball in the viscous stuff. At the last moment he spots it falling out of the fog and runs in to make a spectacular diving catch. By the ninth, however, you can no longer see the infield from the warning track of the outfield. Mel Hall leads off for the Yanks with a fly ball to left. Bradley finally sees, slides, and makes another amazing catch. After a Jesse Barfield single, Milacki is replaced with Kevin Hickey. He walks Steve "Bye Bye" Balboni, and Mark Williamson comes in for Hickey. A Don Slaught single loads the bases. Pinch hitter Ken Phelps then hits a routine fly ball to left. Bradley searches the fog, but never finds the ball. It drops directly behind him for a two-run single and the Birds lose 2-1. It is a crushing defeat, the kind that sticks with you for weeks, the kind that many teams look back on and say, "That's the game. We never quite recovered after that game."

The next night, Jeff Ballard attempts to help the O's forget the heartbreaking loss. He begins by giving up five hits to the Yankees first seven batters. The O's best pitcher seems to have lost it. The walls are caving in. The end appears imminent. Then it happens again. With Balboni at the plate, the Yankees start their runners. Steve hits a line shot that is grabbed by Cal Ripken. He flips to brother Bill to double Steve Sax off second. Billy turns to find Don Mattingly running toward him. He takes a few steps in his direction, then calmly throws over to Randy Milligan. It is the Birds' first triple play in 10 years. It is the first AL triple play of the season. It turns what appeared to be a disastrous inning into a slim 1-0 Yankee lead. In the fourth inning, Cal blasts his fifth home run of the year to tie it up. But the Yanks come right back to go ahead 2-1. The Orioles are on the verge of another agonizing defeat, one that surely will permanently scar this young team. In the bottom of the eighth, down by one, big Randy "Moose" Milligan baffles the Yanks by stealing second. Traber pinch-hits, comes through with a big single, and the game is tied. It goes to the 10th. Tettleton doubles, which brings up Rene Gonzales who is in an 0 for 8 slump, hitless in two weeks.

In a season of amazing performances from unexpected sources, Gonzo does it again, singling home Mickey after Mark Thurmond and Gregg Olson had held the Yanks scoreless over the last three innings. In one game, the awesome emotional letdown of the previous night is gone. It takes a triple play, a surprise stolen base, and a clutch hit from an unlikely source to win. For the first time all season, a few people outside Baltimore start to wonder if maybe there is something to these Orioles. "I don't know if this is the biggest win of the season because we've had some big ones," Frank Robinson says. "But it's a big one, especially after the way we lost that one Wednesday night. It answers some more questions about this team. People have said let's see how they handle adversity, how they come back from a tough loss. This team is starting to answer questions like that."

They certainly are. To close out the home stand, they have an opportunity to show more of that resiliency against the AL champion Oakland A's. Friday night, the 16th, is a double-header to make up one of the rain-outs in May. Brian Holton is hit hard for five runs in five innings, giving up the first home run by an Oriole pitcher in 71 innings. The Birds rally, but fall short, losing 7-5.

In game two the surprising Jay Tibbs may be in over his head this time. He is facing Mike Moore, the AL ERA leader at 1.91. But the Birds steal their way to a few runs, and Tibbs scatters six hits over seven innings. The defense saves the day again, highlighted by Joe Orsulak's diving catch off the bat of Stan Javier in the third inning. The Birds do it again, beating one of the league's best 5-1. "Every time I turned around, one of the outfielders was on his back or stomach making a catch," Tibbs says.

After the game Oakland Manager Tony LaRussa says out loud what some people have begun thinking. "The Orioles are a legitimate team. They will be in the division race."

The next day, Saturday, the O's will compete on national television and get their first opportunity to show the country their legitimacy. Just the fact that national cameras are here gives credibility to this feisty Oriole team. It is the first time in three years that NBC has set foot in Memorial Stadium. J.J. Bautista takes the mound for his first start since being recalled from Rochester. He promptly begins the game by giving up yet another two-run dinger, this time to Mark McGwire. Bautista survives the blast, going on to retire 12 of the last 14 hitters he faces before leaving the game with a torn nail on the index finger of his throwing hand. Phil Bradley is today's offensive hero with two doubles and three RBI's. Mark Williamson and Gregg Olson come in and do it again,

98

shutting down the A's in the seventh, eighth, and ninth to give the Birds a 4-2 victory. Ironically, a rain delay causes NBC to leave the broadcast before it is over, and the nation has yet to see the Orioles win a game.

The Birds' starting pitchers have now gone seven weeks without a complete game. The bullpen is doing an incredible job, and Frank Robinson is using them masterfully. It is obvious, though, that this cannot continue. The Birds are desperate for fresh arms. J.J. Bautista and his chronic blister must return to Rochester immediately after his fine performance. To replace him, the O's call up Mickey Weston, a reliever at Rochester who is 8-2 with a 2.46 ERA.

Mickey gets to Memorial Stadium in time to watch his first major league team score three runs in the first inning on a Bob Melvin double. He then sees Dave Schmidt give up only three hits but two runs over six innings. He watches as the A's lead-off batter in the seventh reaches with a single and Frank Robinson walks slowly to the mound. Frank does not call on the exhausted arm of Mark Thurmond or Mark Williamson or even Kevin Hickey. He calls for him, Mickey Weston. It is a 3-2 game. He is pitching in front of 46,541 seat-squirming fans in Memorial Stadium, 34,000 more people than he has ever pitched in front of before. He comes in with a 2-0 count on Ron Hassey, the go-ahead run. No pressure here. He gets Hassey to knock into a double play, and proceeds to shut out the power-laden A's over the next two innings. In his first major league performance, Mickey saves the day. He promptly becomes the next Bird hero in a season of improbable heroes.

In the ninth, Weston, like all Oriole pitchers, is assisted by two dazzling defensive plays. This time they are both made by Billy Ripken, and one of the two will remain in the memory banks of Oriole fans for a long time. Dave Parker hits a grounder up the middle, past the lunge of Mickey Weston. Billy runs behind the mound, bare hands the ball and in the same motion throws in the general vicinity of first base as his body goes the other direction. Only when he hears the roar of the crowd does Billy realize he has nipped Parker at first. It may have been the finest Billy Ripken play in a career of great defense. As the game ends the O's newest fairy tale producer, Mickey Weston, is met by his manager. The determined look on Weston's face is replaced by a broad smile as Frank jokingly whispers in his ear. "We're sending you back now. We need another fresh arm." The team that Tony LaRussa referred to as "legitimate" has just taken three of four from the acknowledged best team in the AL, his Oakland A's. For the first time this season the A's suffer a three-game losing streak. At 37-28 now, the O's are five games up on the AL East.

Monday, June 19, the Birds travel cross-country for a three-game series with Seattle. In game one, the Birds are sluggish, possibly suffering from a little jet lag. Milacki gives up a three-run home run, leaves the bases loaded in the first, one on in the second, two in the third, and on and on. Somehow, he stays in the game. The O's get two runs when they are in a position to score five. So here they are, playing poorly, but only losing, 3-2. That is the difference in 1989. The good defense keeps them in the game. In the seventh the Birds break through. Finley singles, steals second; Bradley walks; Cal homers; Tettleton homers, etc. By the time the inning is over, it is 9-3. In 1988, the Orioles would have lost this game.

Tuesday, June 20, Jeff Ballard is racked again for five runs in the first inning. He has now allowed 41 base runners in 17

2/3 innings since being hit by Incaviglia. In the second, Billy Ripken hits into a double play with the bases loaded. But you can just "feel" that the Orioles will come back. And back they come with one in the third, three in the fourth, and four in the fifth with big hits contributed by Craig Worthington, Billy Ripken, and Mike Devereaux. The new fairy tale kid, Mickey Weston, comes in to pitch four innings of two-hit ball, getting his first major league win, and the Birds roar back, 8-6.

Game three brings Jay Tibbs back to the mound, another fairy tale maker. His team bats around in both the second and fifth innings. Tibbs shuts out the Mariners through seven before tiring badly in the eighth. A very tired Mark Thurmond comes in and cannot stop Seattle, so Frank must go back and get Gregg Olson, something he did not want to do. But Gregg does the job again, and the O's win 8-6. Tibbs is 4-0 with a 1.79 ERA. Somehow, though, Frank must get some rest for his weary bullpen. But his team has won six in a row again. Since May 16 they are 25-9. At 40-28, they have now taken a seven-game lead on the struggling Eastern division. You have to go all the way back to the powerful 1979 Orioles to find a Baltimore team with a better record after 68 games, and back another decade for a Bird team with a bigger lead at this point in the season. The O's have now been in first place for 26 straight days. Amazing.

The pattern continues in California. Brian Holton is racked after just five innings, blowing a 5-0 Bird lead. But in the eighth, Jim Traber hits his fourth longball of the year; the bullpen does it again, and the O's win 6-5. There is bad news, however. Mickey Weston, the new hero, pitching for the third time in five days, pulls a shoulder muscle. He must return to Rochester while J.J. Bautista comes to Baltimore one more time. The bullpen has saved the last six straight games, a streak believed to be the longest in Oriole history.

Since the loss in the fog at Memorial Stadium against the Yankees, the Birds have won eight of nine games and seven straight. They have not only bounced back from adversity, but seem to have benefited from the experience.

California stops the Oriole express in the rest of the series. Frank Robinson allows his weary bullpen to rest in game two as Dave Schmidt goes all the way in a 5-1 loss. The scary stuff comes in the next two when Jeff Ballard is shelled again and J.J. Bautista gives up three more home runs in five innings. Clearly, J.J. is not pitching to Oriole standards and cannot stay at the major-league level. But how many more heroes can there possibly be lurking in the shadows of Rochester? Another big question: How can the O's win without Ballard? There are discussions about going out of the system for pitchers. Richard Dotson, recently released by the Yankees, is considered, but Frank Robinson and Roland Hemond are not panicking. They refuse to mortgage the future or demoralize the kids that are working so hard to get to the majors.

The O's come home to play Toronto. The Blue Jays have gone 24-14 since Jimy Williams was fired and replaced by interim Manager Cito Gaston, who is now permanent Manager Cito Gaston, if there is any such thing. Cito is attempting to mold his talent-laden squad into a team. Frank Robinson is trying to save his wavering pitching staff, but the press sees something different. June 27, 1989, will be the first time two black managers will oppose each other in the history of baseball. It is sad that such a distinction need be made at all. But as long as reporters find it necessary to ask moronic questions like, "How will you change your managing style against another black manager?'' someone will find it necessary to distinguish between races. Hopefully, that time is coming to a swift conclusion.

The game itself proves to be a weird one. The O's explode for 16 runs, but are out-hit by the Jays when Frank leaves Jay Tibbs in to pitch a complete game. Tibbs pitches a nifty 13-hitter, winning 16-6, and making his record 5-0. Randy Milligan nearly hits four home runs, and ends up settling with two in a 4 for 5 evening with four RBI's. Most importantly, the relief corps gets a well-deserved rest.

The next night is a more normal affair, a classic Oriole performance. Brian Holton goes the normal distance for an Oriole starter, six innings. He gives up just one run on six hits. Kevin Hickey then comes in to kill a seventh-inning rally, keeping another nail-biter tied at 1-1. Gregg Olson also comes up with a masterful performance, striking out the side in the ninth inning with his ''Golden Hammer.'' But the offensive hero this night will be a guy Oriole fans thought would be their only hero in 1989. Cal Ripken, Jr. takes his turn carrying the load, blasting an eighth-inning home run to win it 2-1. It is a classic Oriole win with President George Bush in attendance. The country's chief-executive is now tagged as the O's good luck charm, with the Birds going 3-0 in games which he has attended. Unlike the rest of us, however, George leaves before Cal hits the game-winner, just as he did on opening day.

Before the month ends, Toronto salvages the final game of the series, beating up on Dave Schmidt and J.J. Bautista once again. The next night the Tigers continue the shelling against Bob Milacki and the new kid from Rochester, ''Texas'' Mike Smith. ''Texas'' has been called up to replace an injured Mark Williamson. Oriole fans begin to worry. The staff is failing. The relievers have been carrying the team, and now their new star, Mickey Weston is hurt, as is Mark Williamson, an integral component on this team. Their best starter is getting bombed. No one in the starting rotation can complete a game.

But the month ends, and the sheer overwhelmingness of what is happening convinces the fans that somehow, someway, Frank will find another magician, another hero, another star performance in what can only be described as a fairy tale season. Not only are these Birds not in last place where they are supposed to be, but they are competitive. Not only are they competing, they are winning. Not only are they 43-33, but they are in first place. And not only are they in first place, but they are 5 1/2 games up.

The season rolls on and the heroes just keep coming, each more improbable than the one before. The starters falter in June, and along comes journeyman Jay Tibbs with a lifetime 4.22 ERA going 5-0 with a 2.45 ERA. Then there is Mickey Weston, a guy who had never thrown a single pitch in the majors, demonstrating a fantastic sinker, saving his first game, and winning the second. Mark Huismann, released by the Tigers in spring training, does the same. Kevin Hickey, cut by no less than four major league teams, has come in to retire Wade Boggs, George Brett, and Don Mattingly seven straight times. Left-handers are hitting 4 for 31 against him. Mark Thurmond, a guy who went two calendar years without a victory, has stranded 28 of the 32 runners he has inherited. Mark Williamson, a "throw-in" minor leaguer in the Storm Davis trade with the Padres, is 5-0 with two saves and a 1.08 ERA in his last 16 appearances. Then there is the biggest surprise of all, the kid from Auburn, Gregg Olson. Everyone thought that Olson would eventually be a good major leaguer, but he is not supposed to be here yet. In the month of June he has a 0.57 ERA in 15 2/3 innings. He allowed just six hits and four walks, striking out 19 and immediately becoming one of the most feared closers in baseball.

There is Craig Worthington, a guy who was not supposed to hit, leading AL rookies in RBI's, and coming up with clutch hits for the Birds time after time. Phil Bradley, with a so-called "attitude problem" in Philadelphia and Seattle, is quietly becoming the most consistent player on the team, and at the same time becoming a leader and an inspiration for the rookies. Steve Finley, Mike Devereaux, and Brady Anderson each take their turn as the rookie making another diving catch, stealing another base, and scoring another big run. Randy Milligan, who never got an opportunity to prove himself in New York or Pittsburgh, leads the team in on-base percentage at .433 and plays flawless defense. Then, of course, there is "The Looper," Mickey Tettleton. On this team of illogical success stories, Tettleton is the most incredible. He is the center of the miracle in a baseball season that has become much more than "EXCITING TIMES." With 18 home runs, his name remains at the top of the AL list—this from a guy who finished last in a home run hitting contest at his alma mater, Oklahoma State. He finished behind Pete Incaviglia, Robbie Wine, Gary Green, Doug Dascenzo, and a graduate assistant.

Yes, this is pure fantasy, and there is no longer any sense in attempting to be logical. Of course this cannot last; of course the Birds cannot keep playing like this; of course it will all end. But then everything that has occurred already has been just as impossible.

Frank does not want his team thinking about such things.

"I don't see the standings. I do not hear anything you're saying about them." The fans, however, begin catching a disease they have not experienced for six years. It is pennant fever, and it is sweeping the town, impossible to avoid even for non-baseball fans. There are signs and posters everywhere, but none quite so descriptive as the one in the Owings Mills Mall, on the wall of the athletic shoe store. There, next to the Froot Loops box: **ORIOLES MAGIC NUMBER - 83.**

CHAPTER TEN

Will the Real Orioles Please Stand Up?

Geroge Steinbrenner will never understand. What makes a team win? The best athletes? The highest paid athletes? A conglomeration of the best players money can buy? If you took the ten best pitchers in the game and the 14 best hitters by position and put them all on one team, would they obliterate their competition? You might think by now that the owners of major league franchises would understand that talent does not insure success, that a combination of the best players in the game does not necessarily equal the best team in baseball.

In the years following their 1983 championship, the Orioles fell into the same trap as their rivals. The O's payroll skyrocketed with the addition of free agents, and they soon had the fifth-highest payroll in the game. They also finished in last place.

Unlike the Yankees, however, the Orioles realized their mistake. They went back to the team concept. They began building again from within. They looked as much for desire in a player as they did ability. They wanted enthusiasm and heart. They stopped reaching for the quick fix.

Now, as the 1989 Orioles are closing in on the halfway point of the season, they see desire and heart and a team with a unique chemistry that cannot be purchased at any price. Ironically, all this has happened in less than a year. The Orioles were hoping to be competitive in three years. They gave up the quick fix and instead got a quick fix. The difference is this team is young and will be around for quite some time. At the same time the Orioles now have the lowest payroll in baseball. Dead last. "But many that are first shall be last; and the last shall be first." (Matthew 19:30). If you haven't figured it out by now, George, we are certainly not going to explain it to you.

Meanwhile, Oriole home attendance is setting some records of its own. On June 28, the O's went over the one million mark. When you attend an Orioles game now you will usually see the kind of crowd you used to see only on give-away nights. July 1 happens to be team photo night, and 39,943 show up. But that same amount, give or take a few thousand, has been in the park every night this week and, of course, why not? "THESE ARE EXCITING TIMES," you know. "YOU GOTTA BE THERE."

This July 1 crowd, waving their team photos, has much to get excited about. Their team is winning another tightly contested game against the Detroit Tigers. In the bottom of the sixth it is 2-1. But then Cal Ripken drives a fastball deep to left. Is it fair? Is it fair? YES! An inning later Craig Worthington clears the left field wall again and it is 4-1. In the eighth, the Birds break it open, scoring four, and the fans go berserk again. Their magical O's win 8-1. But the most exciting thing is seeing Jeff Ballard return to his old form, going 7 1/3 innings of 5-hit ball. Hopefully, a mechanical flaw in Ballard's delivery, spotted by pitching coach Al Jackson, will be the answer to Jeff's recent problems. It certainly appears to be the answer tonight.

On Sunday, though, the pitching roof caves in again. The amazing 5-0 Jay Tibbs must leave the game in the fourth inning with what later is diagnosed as tendonitis. The guy who has kept the O's afloat for the last six weeks must now go on the disabled list. Frank Robinson, already juggling a worn-out pitching staff, now has what appears to be an insurmountable problem. The O's also lose the game itself, chiefly due to a curious call by home-plate umpire Ted Hendry in the eighth inning. With Craig Worthington at the plate and two runners on with one out, slow-footed Mickey Tettleton takes off and steals third base, setting up the O's to score, at least the tying, and potentially the winning run. Hendry, however, calls Worthington for catcher interference, sending Tettleton back to second and calling Craig out. When Robinson goes out to argue he is told that the rules require the batter to make an attempt to get out of the catcher's way, which Robinson argues vehemently. Rule 6.06C actually states that a batter may be called out for "any... *movement* that hinders a catcher's play." After the game, Hendry revises his story to say "There was an unnatural movement." So in one day the Birds lose their best pitcher and a game they could have won.

To close out the series and the home stand the O's break out their bright orange jerseys for the first time in 1989, just for a change of pace. They go on to supply an "orange crush" to the Tigers, scoring in each of the first six innings to win 11-4. "The Pumpkin Squad," as Mickey Tettleton dubs them, goes 6 1/2 games up on the division, assuring that

109

they will become the sixth team in history to go from last place one year to first place at the All-Star break. None of those other five, by the way, went on to win their division.

It is the 4th of July, and baseball tradition says whoever is in first on the 4th will be there in October. The national media sits up and takes notice, and before the O's head to Toronto, Frank Robinson appears on ABC's "Good Morning America." Opposite him on NBC's "Today," are two of his players. "The Looper," Mickey Tettleton, and "The Otter," Gregg Olson, are being interviewed. No Oriole appears on CBS, and, incredibly, the network cannot understand why it is last in the morning ratings.

Everyone arrives in Toronto for the Orioles first look at the futuristic Skydome. No one can quite understand why this powerful Blue Jay squad is not crushing their competition in the AL East. But they are not, and the O's take two of three on the Blue Jay's new turf. In game one, Dave Schmidt flirts with a no-hitter for the second time this season. He settles for a combined two-hitter with Mark Williamson and the Birds win 8-0. Game two, the official halfway point of the season, is symbolic of the new Orioles. Eight different players contribute for a total of 13 hits; the brothers' Ripken turn three big double plays, one of which has to be seen to be believed, and Gregg Olson comes in to get his 13th save to preserve a 5-4 victory. Since May 17, the Birds have the best record in the majors (32-15). During this time frame, Gregg Olson and Mark Williamson are 5-1 with 13 saves and a 1.30 ERA.

Milwaukee is the last stop before the break. Pete Harnisch has returned to replace the injured Jay Tibbs in the first game. He is hit hard, and the Birds lose 6-4, despite a Phil Bradley two-run triple and a Cal Ripken two-run dinger.

The concerns about the pitching staff increase each day.

Phil Bradley continues his hot hitting in game two as the Birds win 5-2, but the action builds to a crescendo in the last game before the All-Star break. The O's lose 7-2, but the problems come in the fifth inning when Phil Bradley is called for interference after sliding into Jim Gantner at second base. Just like a week ago, Robinson is angered by the fact that John Shulock changes his story after the game. On the field he tells Frank that Gantner had the ball before Bradley hit him. Frank tells him that there is nothing illegal about that. Afterwards, Shulock tells reporters that Bradley arrived before the ball (the only way rule 7.09G could be properly invoked). Frank is so upset he says, "I'm seriously thinking about stepping aside....I can't manage this ballclub the way things are going. I can't go out and defend my team. I can't question a call....You tell me how I can manage. It's not fair to these players and it's not fair to the people I work for." Those who know Frank Robinson are sure that this is no idle comment.

During the All-Star break, American League President Bobby Brown meets with Frank. He listens to the complaints, the biggest of which is that umpires tell him one thing on the field and tell another to reporters later. Frank is satisfied with Brown's response. By coincidence, the same umpiring crew that was in Milwaukee will open the second half in Baltimore. "We'll find out if things are going to be any different right quick, won't we?" Frank says.

In the All-Star game itself, O's fans get to see two of their players. Cal Ripken is chosen for shortstop, his sixth straight performance in the game. Mickey Tettleton, second in the American League in home runs with 20 is also chosen. Mickey, of course, is not the choice of the fans. Remember,

111

these are the same fans that voted a retired player (Mike Schmidt) and a guy who has not played in one game this year (Jose Canseco) to the squad. Oriole fans were hoping to also see Jeff Ballard (10-4) on the team. But few people outside of Baltimore believe that Jeff is anything but a mirage that will quickly disappear in the second half of the season.

The O's are 48-37, 5 1/2 games up in the AL East. In 1988, they were 28-59 at the break, a 21-game improvement. No team since 1933 has shown greater improvement from one All-Star break to the next. None. Their batting average has gone from .228 to .260, this from a team that was supposed to be weaker offensively. Their ERA has dropped nearly a full point, from 4.73 to 3.81. The O's have improved in virtually every offensive and defensive category, save one. Home runs. In 1989 the O's have two less dingers than in '88, but they have scored over 100 more runs. It's amazing what a little speed and a few sacrifices can do. The pitching has obviously improved dramatically, but much of the success must be attributed to defense. The O's continue to lead the majors in fewest errors and fewest unearned runs allowed.

Can the O's and Frank Robinson continue the first half success in a stretch drive with a wounded pitching staff? Not likely, but of course nothing was ever likely on this team. The second half begins like the first. Frank holds a team meeting. He reminds his young players what got them here. Each game is a new season. Play the game you are in; don't replay the last one; don't look ahead. This is a year of one-game seasons. Not once has Frank discussed anything about a pennant race. He does not start now.

There will be some minor personnel changes. Randy Milligan will probably get an opportunity to play more in the second half, as will Mike Devereaux. Frank thinks they both will hit better playing on a regular basis. Mickey Tettleton may do some designated hitting when he isn't catching to keep his bat in the lineup. Who will pitch? Frank does not know; he only knows that he must find a way to use his bullpen less than in the first half. There had been some hope that the number one pick in the June draft, LSU's Ben McDonald, might step right into a spot in the Oriole rotation, but the brightest prospect in the country has yet to sign with the Orioles. Even if he were to agree to terms in the next week, it is doubtful he could be ready to pitch at the major league level even by September. There seems to be no pitching answer on the horizon.

The O's open at home versus the team with the best record in the major leagues, the California Angels. The Halos trounce the O's in game one 13-5, and the country is immediately convinced that the long awaited Oriole collapse has begun. Oriole fans are also slightly uneasy, but they show up en masse to support their team. 45,921 screaming people show up for game two. The Birds respond with three runs in the second, but the killer comes in the third. Mike Devereaux comes to the plate with the bases loaded. Kirk McCaskill has retired the last two batters, and he is almost out of the jam. Devereaux is struggling at the plate. He is 1 for his last 23. But he smacks a low fastball back up the middle; two runs score, and it is 5-1. The Angels come roaring back, and Gregg Olson is inserted again to put out the fire. In the eighth inning he brings everyone to the edge of their seats. He throws seven straight balls to load the bases. Frank Robinson slowly walks to the mound. He does not pull Gregg out, or even tell him how to pitch to the next batter. Instead, he removes his baseball cap and asks Gregg

113

to examine the new gray hairs he has given him. Olson then gets Devon White to pop up and Wally Joyner to watch one of his vintage curve balls for a third strike and the end of a potential rally. Olson goes on to get his 15th save in 15 tries, and the O's win 6-4. "I think he does that on purpose," says Frank, referring to Gregg's propensity for getting himself in hot water before retiring the side. "He's trying to get me on a Rolaids commercial."

The battle with the number one team in baseball goes to Saturday night. The Angels are battling tooth and nail to stay ahead of the Oakland A's in the AL West. They need to win the next two in the worst way. They blast Dave Schmidt for five runs in 5 2/3 innings, and this time the Oriole relievers cannot stop the Angels either. The O's struggle to stay in the game. But each time they come back to get close or tie it up, the Angels explode again. The knock-out punch seems to come in the top of the seventh when the Angels go up 7-3. But in the bottom of the inning, the O's rush right back, scoring on a Steve Finley single and a two-run, pinch-hit triple by Joe Orsulak. Still, they trail 7-6 and the Angels score again in the eighth and still again in the ninth. In the bottom of the ninth the Angels lead 9-7. But with one out there is still some hope in Memorial Stadium when both Mickey Tettleton and Randy Milligan walk. Both advance a base on a wild pitch. Larry Sheets, who has yet to deliver in a pinch-hit situation this year, is sent up to swing for Bob Melvin. Larry takes his place on the hero stand, delivering a clutch single, scoring both runners and tying the game. The crowd is still going nuts as Mike Devereaux comes to the plate. He hits a deep fly ball down the left field line. It is curving, curving, curving, NO! It's a fair ball! HOME RUN! In a game they were never ahead in until the last pitch, the

O's have stolen a victory in what appeared to be a certain defeat. As the 47,000-plus crowd continues cheering, Angels' coach Marcel Lachemann and Manager Doug Rader go berserk at third base, surrounding umpire Jim Joyce. Television replays are inconclusive. In one, the ball appears to hit the foul pole, in another it seems to drift foul. The shot is shown again and again from ten different angles. "It's definitely fair. No, I'm not sure. No one knows for sure." The O's are out-hit in this one, 19 to nine. Mike Devereaux has the biggest hit of his career, and the O's win a game that the fans will be talking about for years to come.

A few hours later the Orioles and Angels must return for a Sunday afternoon game to end the series. Angels' Manager Doug Rader begins the afternoon by walking to home plate with his line-up card, and continuing a "discussion" with umpire Ken Kaiser on the home run call of the night before. Rader is ejected before the game begins, and in so doing he has already pumped up the Baltimore fans to a fevered pitch.

The game itself matches Bob Milacki against Mike Witt. Bob does it again. He gives up just one run in seven innings, but, as usual, his club is losing 1-0. In the bottom of the inning the Birds rally with singles by Tettleton, Sheets, Devereaux, and Traber. It's 2-1. Frank calls on Olson, as usual. But for the first time in 1989, Olson does not get the save. A dying quail single to the opposite field does him in and the game is tied 2-2. Extra innings. In the top of the 11th, the Angels have the bases loaded with two outs. Frank Robinson brings in "Texas" Mike to face Max Venable. Smith has not exactly been a stopper for the Birds, and some fans cannot bear to watch. But "Texas" gets a ground ball, and a collective sigh of relief comes from the crowd. Bottom of the 11th and Cal walks to bring up Mickey Tettleton. He hits a rocket over first base, it curves—fair or foul? FAIR BALL! The ball hits off the right field seats; Cal keeps running. The throw. He's safe! The Orioles win again and the Angels cry foul again. They cannot believe this has happened to them two games in a row. The Orioles are out-hit in all four games of the Angel series, yet they win three of them. It is an incredible turn-around for the kids, especially after getting blown away in game one. They continue to respond in pressure situations and the surrealism of the Oriole season reaches another level. Were they fair or were they foul? The discussions go on in Baltimore for days. Heck, no one talks about business anymore, not even the yuppies. And the memory of these two games will linger long after the discussions end.

Seattle comes to Baltimore next, and game one gives the O's more reason for rejoicing. They win again 8-4, but the big news is Pete Harnisch. He pitches 8 1/3 innings and gets his first major league victory. It is the longest outing by an O's starter since June 27, and the Bird brass wonders if maybe, just maybe, Harnisch might not be part of the answer to the pitching woes. The victory means that Oriole rookies now have earned a victory or a save in exactly half of the team's 52 wins.

Tuesday, July 18. Oriole fans cannot believe what is happening. Tettleton and Milligan both hit solo home runs, and Craig Worthington adds a two-run shot, his second in as many nights. But in the eighth inning it is 4-3. Greg Briley is on first for Seattle when Darnell Coles hits a blast to left center off Gregg Olson. Briley is off with the pitch on a hit and run and has already scored when he sees the ball skip over the fence for a ground-rule double. Briley must go back to third. Then, with the bases loaded, Craig Worthington fields a change-of-pace grounder. It bounces off his glove; he recovers quickly, and unleashes a rocket to first base, just nipping Dave Valle. Magically, the Birds win again 4-3. "Another laugher," says Mickey Tettleton. The O's are 53-38, 7 1/2 games up on the New York Yankees. They are 15 games over .500 for the first time since 1982. They have just won another five in a row.

The O's lose the last game of the series 7-0, as Brian Holton is rocked for five runs in just two innings. They must now embark on a 14-game road trip, the O's longest road trip in several years. It is a big topic of conversation. The O's try to downplay the significance of the trip. "I think people are making this out to be the only road trip of the year," says Mickey Tettleton. It may not be the only one, but it certainly is the longest, and it is coming at a critical time for the pitching-short Orioles. It also must start in Oakland, where Jose Canseco has just rejoined the A's.

The O's lose game one to the best pitcher in baseball since 1987, Dave Stewart. The final is 5-2. Game two sends "Hard Luck" Milacki up against Mike Moore. Just like clockwork Bob goes out and pitches another gem, and his offense struggles mightily. Just like last week he is losing 1-0, this time in the eighth. A two-out Oriole rally with consecutive hits by Bradley, Finley, Ripken, Jr., and Tettleton brings the Birds back. It is 2-1, so Frank calls on the stopper. This time though, Gregg cannot nail it down. He walks four men; the A's score twice, and the O's lose the kind of game they have won nearly every time this year.

The next night, Pete Harnisch pitches well again, but the offense sputters, and the effort is wasted as the Orioles lose 3-1. On Sunday the good pitching continues. Jeff Ballard pitches a much needed complete game and gives up just four

117

hits. Steve Finley and Joe Orsulak both make leaping catches at the wall on consecutive at-bats. Cal hits a two-run homer. The O's out-hit the A's six to four. But still, the O's lose 3-2. It is a frustrating series. The O's play well; their starting pitching returns, but they are swept.

More bad news arrives when the Birds find out that Jay Tibbs, expected back any day, now must go on the 21-day disabled list. But there is no panic in these Birds. While the national media has again predicted their collapse, they know they have played well during this five-game losing streak.

The Birds do not play well in Minnesota, however. They lose game one 9-3, when Kirby Puckett breaks open a close game in the fifth with a three-run homer. The next night, though, is Bob Milacki's turn. The O's are determined to score some runs for him this time and come out swinging with four runs in the first inning. Things look great, but the Birds never score again. The Twins battle back, and this time the winning run scores against Mark Williamson as the Birds lose 5-4. Suddenly the Oriole relief squad has fizzled. Have they reached their limit? Have the frequent appearances caught up with them?

In the last game of the Minnesota series Pete Harnisch has nothing. The O's lose 10-6, and now everyone is jumping on the bandwagon, certain that this is the end for the Baby Birds. Baltimore fans turn philosophical, "They gave us a great season as long as they could. It was fun while it lasted."

The O's have lost eight in a row. They are now 53-46. What was a 7 1/2 game lead is now four. Surely it is just coincidence that all of these losses have come just as the O's won 53 games. Surely this can have nothing to do with the fact that in the disaster year of 1988 the team won a grand total of 54 games. Surely the Birds will win two more games, won't they?

The unfriendly confines of Royals' stadium are next on this disastrous road trip. If ever there was a place where the Orioles are unlikely to snap a losing streak, Royals' stadium must surely be that place. Jeff Ballard takes the mound against Mark Gubicza, and Ballard gives the O's just what they need. He pitches 8 1/3 innings of six-hit ball, giving up no walks. Gregg Olson is handed the ball in the ninth with a 3-1 lead. Oriole fans sit in front of the television in a daze as their rookie sensation gives up three hits and two walks, blowing his third save in the last four opportunities, and the game is tied 3-3. Mark Williamson does come in to stop the Royals as the game goes on and on, now headed into the 13th inning. The sure-armed Bob Boone then unleashes a wild throw from behind the plate into center field. Orsulak scores all the way from second, and in strange fashion the losing streak is over.

The win does not turn the O's around, however. Before the month ends they lose the next two to K.C. 5-0 and 7-6. They can do no better in Fenway, losing to the Red Sox 9-6. The O's have lost 11 of their last 12. What began as some tough losses has turned into a major disaster. The offense has been sporadic, but the real killer is the relief pitching. Certainly the relievers could not be expected to bail out the Orioles for the remainder of the year, but without them the Birds are in serious trouble. In addition, the incredible defense is slipping for the first time. In the last game of the month, they make a season high four errors and give up four unearned runs. It took them 39 games to give up their first four unearned runs. They are now 54-49, a meager three games up on Toronto and Boston. They can now lose their hold on first place in Boston. The Orioles are, in short,

119

coming apart at the seams.

They made their only concession to the pennant race three days ago by trading a young pitching prospect, Brian DuBois, to the Detroit Tigers for the solid hitting Keith Moreland. Moreland is a career .281 hitter. He is hitting .299 for the Tigers, and the O's are hoping he can do the same for them down the stretch. Earlier in the month, Roland Hemond traded minor league pitcher John Habyan to the Yankees for another fleet-footed outfielder named Stanley Jefferson.

The biggest concern, though, is pitching. The choice is made to call up a 29-year-old starter at Rochester named Dave Johnson. Johnson is 7-6 at AAA with a 3.26 ERA. He has never started a major league baseball game. It sounds like a desperate move, but then, these are desperate times. If there was ever a time for a miracle, this is it.

CHAPTER ELEVEN

Why Not?

Perspective. That's the word. Keep things in perspective. This is not 1988. The Orioles have proven time and again they are not that baseball team. Things will settle down. "This, too, shall pass." The Orioles' retired radio and television broadcaster, Chuck Thompson, used to have a saying for these situations. "You are never as good as you look when you're winning, and never as bad as you look when you're losing." Perspective.

As the Orioles lose both ends of a double-header in Fenway to open the month, it now seems impossible that they can recover. They are just too young; they have absolutely no experience with such things. Frank Robinson, more than anyone else, realizes how scarring this disaster has been. All he can do is attempt to remain as calm and poised as possible. He is doing an amazing job at both, something he could never have done in his managing days at Cleveland or San Francisco. The youngsters look at their manager and see no fear, nothing reactionary. It is the only constant that

121

makes them think this ordeal may end.

The O's have now lost five straight, and 13 of their last 14. If they lose again tonight, they will fall out of first place for the first time since May 26. It is the final game of a road trip that will haunt Oriole fans for a long, long time. You get the feeling that as soon as the Orioles do lose, the season will be over. Once they actually fall out of first place there will be nothing left to buoy the kids. They will sink like an anchor to sixth place. Hopefully Detroit will spare them the agony of finishing last again.

No one is actually panicking, but the attitude is obviously miles apart from that seen in the O's dugout and clubhouse two weeks ago. Has it only been two weeks? It seems like two months. The kids are no longer loose; you can feel the tension. Mickey Tettleton expresses the Oriole mood succinctly. "I don't think it's really down; it's more like bewildered." Exactly.

The dreaded game begins. The BoSox score. They score again, then again, and again. It is 6-0. The innings painfully drag on, still the O's cannot put up a single tally. Oriole fans, watching at home, do not turn off their televisions; that would not be very Oriole-like. But many find something moist in their eyes. It has been quite an emotional season, and they cannot stand to see this happen to their kids. It is like watching a family member in deep pain, with no way to help them bear it. The Oriole dugout is catatonic. Cal Ripken, Sr. shouts in from the third base box, "THIS IS FENWAY! ANYTHING CAN HAPPEN!" The place remains dead. Frank Robinson is desperate. He picks up the bullpen phone and calls for the 33-year-old with the emotional makeup of a hyperactive 10-year-old, the Cinderella kid, Kevin Hickey. Brian Holton has just entered the game, so Hickey is a mite confused by the call. He obediently follows orders, however, and comes down to the dugout. "What do you want?" Hickey asks Robinson.

"Liven up this morgue," says Frank.

So with Hickey leading cheers, the Orioles try again to get something going in the top of the 6th. Finally, there is a spark. Mickey Tettleton hits one high and deep to left, up and over the green monster. Newly acquired Keith Moreland singles. Craig Worthington doubles. Billy Ripken hits a bouncer to second, dives into first base, and just beats the throw. It's 6-2. Before the inning ends, Mike Devereaux singles to score Worthington. It is 6-3, and Oriole fans allow themselves the opportunity to feel alive for an inning. Brian Holton has stopped the Red Sox attack in the mid-innings, so the Bird offense tries again in the seventh. Cal singles; Tettleton walks. Keith Moreland, who has three hits already, flies out. That brings up Randy Milligan. In three previous at bats with Moreland on in front of him, Milligan has been unable to deliver. As Moreland returns to the bench he looks over at Randy. "This is your time." Milligan nods. He then strokes a towering fly ball to right-center. It goes up and over the bullpen, and suddenly, the game is tied. Oriole fans at home have strewn popcorn all over their living rooms. The Oriole dugout is back, supercharged. In one pitch the season has turned again. Of course it is just tied, but everything "feels" more like it did two weeks ago.

In the eighth, Phil Bradley scores on a Cal Ripken double. Cal scores on a Milligan sacrifice fly, and Craig Worthington comes through again, singling home Mickey Tettleton. The O's win 9-8. They erase a six-run deficit, their biggest comeback of the season, and one of the biggest in team history. It comes on a night when they would have fallen out

123

of first place without the win. It is a HUGE win, the kind of game young teams never win. The *Associated Press* describes the win as "almost inconceivable." The Orioles send a message to the AL East. "We are not leaving without a fight." Maybe these kids will not pull off the storybook win of the century, but they have proven that they are a team with moxie. No, it is more than moxie. There really is no word to describe it. Our neighbors to the south would call it *ganas*, and that probably comes closest. If ever there was a baseball team with *ganas*, the 1989 Baltimore Orioles must certainly be it. It is a stunning way to end "the trip," and that is the other bonus. "The trip" is over, and the Birds are coming home to their "fantastic fans." Those fans will do their utmost to help them forget the most agonizing weeks of the season.

The Rangers are in town, and here comes President Bush again to witness his fourth Oriole game. While George's record is 3-0, Oriole fans want to know who he is rooting for tonight. His son does own the Texas Rangers, after all. By the end of the game, O's fans are hoping George is planning a trip to the USSR and stays there until the baseball season is over. The O's are losing 6-2, but after the President has once again left the stadium, the Orioles come rushing back. They score two in the ninth and the bases are loaded with Mickey Tettleton at the plate. Tettleton strikes out, and the Birds lose 6-4. The next day fans learn that Mickey was playing hurt. Mickey Tettleton, central figure in the Oriole turn-around, tied for fourth in the AL with 22 home runs, has torn the cartilage in his left knee. Tettleton definitely will not be able to catch again this season. There is hope that he may be able to return sometime in September in a designated hitter capacity. It is a deep blow to the Bird pennant hopes. If they have done anything, however, the O's have proven they are far from quitters. It is clear now that no one is going to give up.

There is some talk of using Keith Moreland behind the plate. Chris Hoiles may be called up from Rochester. Instead, the Orioles sign free agent Jamie Quirk, a 15-year veteran with excellent defensive skills. While Quirk is weak at the plate, Frank Robinson will not abandon the one constant that has kept the Orioles on top. Defense. Someone else will have to pick up the offense. Bob Melvin will become the full-time catcher.

The kids go out and show immediately that no one is going to curl up and die. They take the next two from the Rangers, beating Nolan Ryan on Saturday and winning Sunday's game 3-2 in ten innings. Their slim 2 1/2 game lead on the Red Sox holds up.

The Minnesota Twins are the next invaders. In game one the O's find themselves playing without both of their big guns when Cal Ripken, Jr. is thrown out of the game in the first inning. Cal's consecutive playing streak of 1,198 games remains intact, but the ejection may have cost the O's a 4-2 loss on a night when Jeff Ballard is pitching well. It is only Cal's second ejection of his career. Home-plate umpire Drew Coble says his decision to eject Cal "was kind of like throwing God out of Sunday school."

It is now up to rookie Dave Johnson to save the O's. Middle River, Maryland, is ecstatic. Dave Johnson, their hometown boy, is about to live out his lifelong dream. He is pitching in Memorial Stadium, his boyhood wonderland, for his team, the Baltimore Orioles. He has put in 7 1/2 years in the minor leagues. A trade in the spring brought him to the Baltimore organization from Pittsburgh. Now the

125

moment he dreamed about during his days at Overlea High School is about to come true. Johnson throws strikes all night, hitting the corners with pinpoint control. The Twins do not understand why they are not pummeling Johnson. Not only do they not pummel him, they can't even get him out of the game. Dave pitches a complete game, winning 6-1, and over 100 screaming friends and relatives are waiting for Dave after the game.

Mickey Tettleton, Gregg Olson, Jay Tibbs, Mickey Weston, Mark Williamson, Kevin Hickey, Craig Worthington, Mike Devereaux, and now, Dave Johnson. Never has a single sports team had so many Cinderellas. If a Hollywood producer were to write this script, no one would believe it.

In his search for another starter in the rotation, this time to replace the slumping Dave Schmidt, Frank turns to reliever Mark Thurmond. While Thurmond has consistently done the job in relief, he is not the answer in the starting role. He faces just ten batters and gives up five runs as the Birds lose 7-0.

Now it is nail-biter time again. The O's are 58-54, two games up on the Blue Jays and 2 1/2 up on Boston. The Red Sox are coming to town with a chance to take over the division lead. Friday night is another double-header, something the already thin pitching staff must continue to face due to all the early season rainouts. The O's lose 6-4 in game one to Roger Clemens when their ninth inning rally falls short. Game two features Pete Harnisch (1-5 with a 5.55 ERA) versus Mike Smithson. The O's need another improbable performance, this time from struggling Pete Harnisch, or they will have only a 1/2 game lead. All Pete does is pitch his best game ever in the majors. It is a sparkling three-hitter as the O's win 4-1. Most impressive is Pete's control, something he has struggled with all year. He walks just one, and he retires the last 17 in a row against the best hitting club in the AL. Add another name to the Oriole list of fairy tale heroes.

On Saturday night the struggling offense comes around, and the pitching blows up. The O's blow their biggest lead of the season and suffer a crushing 10-8 loss in 13 innings. The last thing the O's needed was another character builder. But on Sunday, it is win or go down to a half game lead again. "If ever there was a game we were going to quit," Oriole first base coach Johnny Oates says, "today would have been the day." The man from Middle River, Dave Johnson, is on the mound again. All six of the Oriole relievers were used in Saturday night's loss. Frank Robinson has no idea who he can put in if Dave Johnson falters. But Dave saves the day again. He stops Boston cold, pitching yet another complete game when the Birds must have one, and the O's win 6-1. Robinson calls Johnson "amazing." Johnson allows just one hit after the third inning, and he retires the last 11 batters of the game. For the second time in a week Johnson comes up with a huge win, and gives the worn-out staff a rest they desperately need. He becomes the first O's pitcher to throw back-to-back, complete-game victories in a year.

The "dog days" of August roll on, and the O's keep coming up with new ways to win. "It's not just enthusiasm," Robinson says. "They've shown a lot of character, a lot of heart. They don't get down on themselves, and they don't get too high. They keep an even keel on their emotions. They let go of the previous game." Yes, yes, we know, but what is going to happen by September? "I don't know what they're going to do," Robinson says. "We're all in uncharted waters. But I don't think anything will get to this ballclub. They may be beat in tough ball games down the stretch. But I don't think they're going to feel the pressure."

Next comes a minor recess in the home stand as the Birds travel to Tiger Stadium. On the way the Birds learn that the Baltimore kid, a volunteer fireman in the off season, Dave Johnson, has been named AL player of the week. Tonight though, Frank has another problem. Who will pitch? On the plane ride, the idea hits him. He puts Brian Holton in to start. Holton pitches well, but after three innings he is removed. Mark Thurmond then throws the next three and Dave Schmidt follows with three more. The conglomerate is facing Jack Morris, and all four pitchers look great. In the fourth, Stan Jefferson, recently called up from Rochester to replace the injury-ridden Brady Anderson, hits his second home run of the year to tie the game 1-1. In the seventh, Thurmond walks Lou Whitaker after retiring all nine of the previous batters he's faced. A chopper over Worthington's head puts Tigers on second and third with no outs. Enter Dave Schmidt. With the infield in, Cal Ripken gobbles up a Tracy Jones grounder. Doug Strange then hits a rocket that is speared by Randy Milligan, a few inches off the ground. Two outs. Schmidt K's Mike Heath and the threat dies. It is still 1-1 and Jack Morris is pitching his best game of the season. In the 10th inning Morris is still pitching when Mr. Clutch, Craig Worthington, does it again. He deposits a three-run homer in the upper deck of right field. Olson comes in for the save, and the O's win 4-1, spoiling a masterful performance by Morris with a pitching-by-committee formula.

The O's take two of three when they split shutouts with the Tigers in the next two. Milacki, with three days rest, pitches a three-hitter and wins 2-0. Then Frank Tanana

128

turns a two-hitter to beat Baltimore 2-0.

Here comes Toronto. The Blue Jays remain just 1 1/2 games behind the Birds and they too come to Memorial Stadium with a chance to knock the O's out of first. So what else is new? In game one the Birds come up with an eight-run fourth inning when Cal Ripken, Jr. blasts a two-run home run in this, his 1208th consecutive game, moving him to third on the all-time list. Stan Jefferson, the new kid on the block, hits a three-run shot of his own and knocks in a career high five runs. Add one more hero to the long list of improbable Oriole success stories as the O's win 11-6.

The Blue Jays come right back to win the next two. Bob Milacki pitches his second consecutive three-hitter, but loses on Saturday as his mates' bats go silent again.

Sunday afternoon, August 20. The Birds are up against the wall one more time. Their lead over both Milwaukee and Toronto is 1/2 game. They have *no* rested pitcher; they are not hitting, and Toronto is throwing their best, Dave Stieb. Only one other team in the history of baseball has gone this far into the season in first place after finishing last the year before. That team was the 1977 Chicago White Sox. Their General Manager was a guy named Roland Hemond. That team fell out of first place for good on this exact day. The situation can only be described as bleak.

Robinson chooses Pete Harnisch to start the biggest game of his career. He must do it on three days rest. In the second inning, the Blue Jays mount the first rally. Tony Fernandez streaks home on a Nelson Liriano single, but Joe Orsulak throws a one-hop strike to the plate. Fernandez beats the throw, but Quirk expertly blocks him from the plate, then applies the tag. The crowd of 37,242 erupts. One batter later Rene Gonzales is running to cover second on an attempted steal. Junior Felix hits a bolt in the opposite direction. Rene leans backwards and makes a tremendous stab to save another run. Two utility players make two unbelievable plays to stop the Jays and set the tone. In the third there is more. Jamie Quirk makes a catch up against the first base seats. Mookie Wilson drag-bunts, but Harnisch makes another sparkling play to nip him at first. In the fourth there is yet more. Fred McGriff, crime dog, and AL home run leader, hits a deep, deep drive to left. Phil Bradley dives— and just catches it in the end of his glove, sprawling across the warning track. In the fifth the Jays are still attacking. They have runners on second and third with no outs. Harnisch strikes out McGriff and the Jays go quietly again.

Larry Sheets comes up with a big offensive day going 3 for 4; Mike Devereaux strokes a home run and the Birds do it again. They beat Stieb; Harnisch comes up with another gutty performance, and the defense does it again. It ends 7-2, but the Blue Jays could just as well have won this one. The big ones are getting impossible to rank in importance. But this one has to be one of the biggest.

Baseball fans are not talking about the astonishing O's however. Instead, the conversations keep bringing up the streaking Milwaukee Brewers. The Brew crew has won nine of their last ten and while the O's have kept the Blue Jays off their back, the Brewers have moved into second. They remain just 1/2 game behind the Birds. This is getting tiring. Now if our Hollywood scriptwriter was penning his mythical season, he would next have the Brewers come to Baltimore for a showdown series. Three guesses who the O's next opponent will be.

Here we go again. One more time the Birds must win or fall out of first. They now have gone longer into the season in first place than any team in baseball history that finished last the previous year. More uncharted waters for the Cinderella kids. This time it is Jeff Ballard's turn. Ballard is pitching with three days rest for the first time. No one knows how he will respond. In the top of the fourth, he shows the 32,000 Oriole faithful what he can do when the chips are down. There are runners on second and third with no outs. The Brewers have their 3-4-5 hitters up next, Glenn Braggs, Robin Yount, and Greg Brock. The Brewers have been knocking the cover off the ball for the last ten days. Ballard is praying he can get out of this with just one run which would leave the game tied. He keeps the ball in on Braggs and gets a pop-up to first. Since Ballard rarely strikes out anyone, a pop-up was his only chance. Robin Yount is next and Ballard employs the same strategy. Robin pops up to second. Greg Brock follows with a ground-out. The stadium is in total bedlam again, and when the players come into the dugout Frank says, "If that doesn't inspire you, nothing will."

Stan Jefferson follows with an inspirational home run, his fourth since joining the O's. In the fifth, more inspiration as Cal delivers a three-run blast. It is 5-0. There is also the great "D." Ballard picks off Glen Braggs. Bradley throws out Robin Yount trying to get a double; Worthington makes a great play from deep behind third; Billy Ripken ranges far to his right to stop a ball on the outfield grass; Cal does the same on a shot in the hole; Devereaux makes one more great catch. Some teams could make their yearly highlight film from the plays the Orioles have made in the last two days. Ballard throws his second complete game of the year and his first shutout of the year. He is the first Oriole to ever throw a shutout without a walk or a strikeout. It is simply another determined Oriole win on another day when they had to

131

win.

It is August 22 and this three-day rest stuff is working so well that Frank decides to keep it up. His young staff of three rookies and a one-year veteran is responding to the challenge magnificently. They are, in fact, pitching better than any time this year. During five starts with three days rest, the starters are 4-1 with three complete games and a 1.76 ERA. Tonight is Dave Johnson's turn. He must face Chris Bosio, who is 14-7 with a 2.55 ERA. He is in the top five in virtually every statistical category. Then there is this new guy, Stanley Jefferson. Not to be outdone by the other outfield gazelles, Stan steals both second and third in the first inning. Joe Orsulak sacrifices him home, and the Birds manufacture an early 1-0 lead. The Birds add three in the second and the defense just keeps on coming. Melvin throws out Yount attempting to steal, Billy Ripken fields a drag-bunt in his glove and shovels it to first in the same motion to get another out. Craig Worthington dives to his left, smothers another one; Traber digs it out at first and Paul Molitor is robbed.

There is a two-hour rain delay, but does that bother the incredible Dave Johnson? He stays right in there, watching Phil Bradley running in during the seventh inning on the wet turf to make another diving, sliding catch. Johnson completes another one; the Birds win 4-2, and the Milwaukee Brewers are shell-shocked. Dave Johnson leads the Oriole pitching staff with three complete games, all, of course, in the last 15 days.

August 23, and the last game of the home stand. Just when things are going nearly perfect, it happens again. Billy Ripken and Craig Worthington are both hurt in the long rain delay game the night before. This is no time to be losing defense and the club's best clutch-hitter. What else can go wrong? The O's make another desperation call to Rochester for infielder Tim Hulett. Tim is leading the International League in doubles and triples, and arrives in time to play third base. Bob Milacki is on the mound and responds again with three days rest. But as usual, he goes into the seventh inning down 1-0. Milacki has now gone into at least the seventh inning 17 times this year and only has six wins to show for it. But in the bottom of the inning Keith Moreland, who only has one RBI in 55 at bats since August 1, delivers with the bases loaded. He strokes a ground-rule double to left and the crowd of 33,000 begins an incessant chant, one that takes them back to 1982 and the final series of the year against these same Milwaukee Brewers. SWEEP! SWEEP! SWEEP! The Birds do sweep. They curtail the hot Brewers right in their tracks. Milwaukee's Glen Braggs says it well. "Man, I can't recall a mistake they made in the series. It's like these three days were a blur."

The O's are burning again. They have won eight of their last 11, fighting off three teams that tried to take over first place in the process.

On to the Bronx for a big five-game series with the Yanks. The O's do just what they hope to do: take four of five. With all the injuries, they need help from some pretty strange sources, but just like all year, they get it. Larry Sheets homers. The newest newcomer, Tim Hulett, homers. Joe Orsulak, a great hitter for average, must muscle up. He hits two home runs. Slow-footed Bob Melvin triples. Jeff Ballard, a guy who rarely strikes out anyone, strikes out Don Mattingly, who has K'd only 19 times the entire season. Ballard does not strike out Mattingly once, he does it twice, and then a third time! The Birds hit and run, sacrifice, manufacture more home runs. The defense makes no less than seven spectacular plays. It causes the Yankee announcers to remark that the only way you can hit one in between the Baltimore outfield is to hit one over the fence.

Off to Cleveland where the Birds lose a heartbreaker 3-1, before rebounding to beat Greg Swindell 7-4. It is the eighth time this year, mostly in the last month, that the O's have played with a game or less lead. It is the seventh time they have won. But the Blue Jays are on fire. They sweep the White Sox and on the last day of the month it finally happens. The O's lose; the Blue Jays win, and for the first time in 97 days the Birds must share first place with another team. They are in a dead heat with Toronto, both at 72-62. Both the O's and the Jays are playing great baseball, and here comes September.

Of course, everyone said it was impossible. They said it over and over. But the Birds are here. September will begin and these astonishing O's will be in a division race. There is a new saying flying around Baltimore. It started in Memorial Stadium, during the sweep of Milwaukee. A banner in the right field bleachers expresses Baltimore's answer to the comments they have heard all year, and are frankly sick of hearing. "The Orioles can't keep this up. They will fold. They can't win with the personnel they have. They can't win with the pitching staff they have. They can't survive the injuries. They can't hold up in a pennant race," and on and on and on. Hence the new banner, "WHY NOT?" It becomes the rallying cry of an entire city. "WHY NOT?" is plastered over the stadium. It becomes a chant during the late innings, an incantation to the heavens. It is printed on T-shirts, and it becomes the number one selling shirt in town. Indeed.

"WHY NOT?"

CHAPTER TWELVE

From Worst to?

Oriole fans look at their calendars. September. They look at the standings in the AL East. They look back at their calendars. Yes, it is September, and yes, the Baltimore Orioles are in the thick of a pennant race. Bird fans have just watched their team pull themselves out of their only slump of the year. Last year they were the very worst. This year they will battle for first. Even Oriole fans still must shake their heads in amazement. They have witnessed the miracle first hand. They know their team is not blessed with the best talent and that they have virtually no experience. But they have seen the blend of youth and enthusiasm jell almost instantaneously into a team. They know that what their players lack in ability, they make up for with drive and determination. They have never seen a team with such resolve, and they have seen some of the best teams of the quarter century. This is a team of overachievers in a town that loves anyone who gives his all. It is the perfect match of a city and a sports team, and the emotional bond that has grown between them has made Baltimore a more vibrant city and the Orioles a more successful team.

It is difficult, if not impossible, for outsiders to understand. The O's begin the month in Chicago, and White Sox announcer Tom Paciorek is one of the many who does not quite get it. The Orioles cleanup batter has six home runs. Their leading hitter is batting .286. Their starting rotation consists of three rookies and a one-year man who had a major league record of 10-20 before the season began. Their bullpen is near exhaustion. They are 12th out of 14 teams in the AL in hitting. They are eighth in pitching. Paciorek echoes the sentiment of the nation. "How can Baltimore be in first?" Oriole fans just smile.

Fans also know, however, that the total lack of hitting recently cannot continue. They are hitting .178 over the last 44 innings, and in that time have not had one extra base hit. Chicago easily takes two of three, and it takes Pete Harnisch's best performance of the year, along with a combination of stolen bases and sacrifices plus two incredible defensive plays, for the Birds to win the middle game of the set 2-1. This means that for the first time in 98 days, the Orioles fall out of first place.

The Birds are in some desperate need of assistance. Mickey Tettleton knows that, and he is busting himself to get back into the lineup. It may only be a few more days. Back on August 19, first-round pick Ben McDonald finally signed a contract. It is probably too late to help this year, but who knows? Stranger things have happened. Rosters can also be expanded now that it is September. Along with Ben McDonald the Birds call up three more pitchers: Curt Schilling, J.J. Bautista, and another of the Cinderella kids, Mickey Weston. Steve Finley has also rejoined the team. His rehabilitation assignment at Hagerstown must have gone well. He hit .417 with the AA team. Brady Anderson is also back along with outfielder Butch Davis, who hit .300 at Rochester. First baseman Francisco Melendez and shortstop Juan Bell come up to assist wherever they can in the infield.

The O's don't need help down the road though; they need it now. They need a spark. A spark, nothing, they need an electrical storm. Fortunately they are heading back to their main power source, Memorial Stadium where 33,000 maniacal fans have decided that they will supply their heroes with a jump start.

It is Labor Day. A dead silence falls over the park as Rex Barney asks for a moment of silence for late Baseball Commissioner Bart Giamatti. Then the national anthem, the cry of "O's!" and the electricity begins. The Birds take the field and there is more fervor than on opening day. Dave Johnson, suddenly tagged with the nickname "Magic," is facing Greg Swindell. Cleveland scores three times in the first, and the way the O's are hitting, this game may already be over. But Mike Devereaux leads off with the Birds first double in 44 innings. Two runs score. In the third, Cal delivers the blast the Birds need desperately, a two-run shot, his 19th of the year. It is the Orioles' first home run in 58 innings. Cleveland gets runners on third in both the fourth and fifth innings, but Johnson wriggles out of both. Yet, in the eighth, Johnson is lifted, and Cleveland ties it up 4-4 when ex-Oriole Mike Young delivers an RBI single. It is the bottom of the ninth and the Oriole bats have gone dead again. Fifteen consecutive batters have been retired. Two outs and Tim Hulett steps up, the minor leaguer called up to play for the injured Billy Ripken and Craig Worthington. Earlier in the year the 29-year-old Hulett, who had played in

137

the majors with the White Sox in '86 and '87, had seriously considered giving up baseball. He was sure he had major league ability and didn't know if he wanted to go out and prove himself all over again at the minor league level. Hulett perservered. Now he has just fouled off five consecutive pitches, battling with everything he has. He drills the next pitch deep to left-center...IT'S GONE! The O's do it again, winning 5-4, and the fans are in euphoria. Hulett now has nine RBI's since joining the team on August 23, the most of any Oriole over that time. He's batting .293 and becomes the latest in an incredible list of improbable Oriole game-savers. "Same old story," cracks first base coach Johnny Oates. "I'm getting tired of seeing it." Meanwhile, the Toronto Blue Jays are winning again. They continue to hold a one-game lead on the Orioles.

Tuesday night, first inning, Cal Ripken sends a drive to left-center. Brad Komminsk is at the fence, leaps, catches the ball, and then disappears over the fence. Cal is awarded his 20th home run of the year; the Birds take a 1-0 lead and Cal is the first shortstop in major league history to hit 20 or more home runs in eight straight seasons. Only later, with the help of a center field camera, it is revealed that Komminsk actually did drop the ball on the other side of the fence. It is termed "the greatest catch never made." In the seventh, Cal comes through again, this time with a double to knock in the go-ahead run. Larry Sheets follows with another double, and the Birds are up 3-1. Just when the O's need them, the veterans come through in the clutch. Bob Milacki and Gregg Olson team to stop the Indians, and the Birds win one more time. But those pesky Blue Jays win also, and the O's cannot pick up any ground.

September 6 is the last game versus Cleveland. Curt

Schilling will make his first start and Ben McDonald his first appearance in the majors. Ben appears because the O's are losing 9-0. McDonald throws well; the crowd gives him a thunderous ovation. Toronto keeps winning. They have now won 14 of their last 16 games and their lead over Baltimore is two. Oriole fans wonder if the Blue Jays will ever lose again; Frank Robinson knows that if his team falls back one more game their miraculous season will probably be over. Frank continues his season-long strategy, "one game at a time." But Oriole fans can't help but look ahead. You try not to, but somehow your eyes keep falling to the same place on the schedule—the final three games of the season against the Jays, in Toronto. Could it be that these O's could come up with enough miracles to set up a storybook finish at the Skydome? Oriole fans have a two-word response. "WHY NOT?"

The Birds travel to Texas for a big five-game series. Of course everything is big now because one false step and the Birds will go crashing down. The big pressure comes on Thursday night. Without enough fresh arms to pitch, the Birds must play a doubleheader, the most important doubleheader of the season. Even a split will be disastrous combined with a Blue Jay win. It has been literally years since the Orioles won both ends of a doubleheader. Now comes the bad news. The Rangers are pitching Nolan Ryan and Bobby Witt. To say their backs are against the wall would be like saying it gets chilly at the North Pole. In game one Nolan Ryan and the Rangers strike out 16 Orioles, but Larry Sheets comes up with one of the biggest games of his season, reaching base five times. Cal gets on four times. Mike Devereaux hits a three-run homer and knocks in two other runs, and the O's don't really care how many times Nolan strikes them out. The rest of the league is hitting .186 against Ryan but the Birds beat him for the third time 8-3. In game two the inexplicable offensive explosion continues. Every player in the lineup gets at least one hit and the O's win 9-6. With the Blue Jays win, the Birds only pick up 1/2 game. But the O's ability to win virtually every critical game shows that they are not going to bow out without a street fight.

The tension is unbearable for Oriole fans. Every game could now represent the end of the season. On Saturday night both the Blue Jays and Orioles go into extra innings. The Birds must battle back to tie. Finally, Randy Milligan hits a dramatic, two-run shot to win for the Birds. Toronto goes 16 innings, and wins again.

On Sunday the O's pitching shortage catches up with them again as they are bombed 8-1. Toronto turns up the heat, winning yet again. The Birds fall 2 1/2 out, three in the loss column. The magical mystery season may be over.

There is some good news, however. The Birds are coming home for 11 big games before finishing the year on the road. O's fans know that now is the time. The Birds must turn it on and the fans plan on doing their part to make it happen. They have done it all year. Attendance has gone over the two million mark at the earliest point in club history. No one is going to let up now. Radio stations all over town are playing a new song entitled "WHY NOT?" The O's are on the lips of people in every walk of life. The O's are doing the undoable and these fans can't stop talking about it. There are banners all over the stadium to represent their feelings. Some have been there much of the year and some are brand new. There are now "official" banners with the new team slogan, "WHY NOT?" but there are many more hand-made versions.

140

Everywhere you look, there it is, on T-shirts and buttons, but that is just the beginning. The outfield is plastered with signs for individual players. There's "PHIL'S PHLOCK," "GREGG'S GROUPIES," "BRADY'S BUNCH." The biggest of them all is for home town boy, Dave Johnson. "HOME TO STAY #27 BALTIMORE'S BEST." There are plenty more. "BALTIMORE IS THE O'S ZONE." Another saying is making the rounds throughout the Oriole region, and that sign, too, is posted. "O BABY, JUST MAYBE!"

Of course, it is not just in the stadium, not even just in Baltimore. All of Maryland is caught up in the Birds, as are much of Virginia, Washington, and North Carolina, plus a nice chunk of Pennsylvania. Everyone is happy, and it is difficult to walk down a street without hearing, "CAN THEY DO IT?" "WHY NOT?" It is all reminiscent of 1982, but because of last year, even better.

The first night of the home stand is Mickey Tettleton's first back in the starting lineup. In Mickey's previous pinch-hit appearances his timing has seemed as off as you might expect after being out for over a month. But in his first at bat tonight "The Looper" strokes a home run to straightaway center. Phil Bradley goes 4 for 4, manufacturing two runs on his own with stolen bases and hustle. O's win 6-3.

On Tuesday and Wednesday nights the division race takes another weird twist. The Blue Jays and Orioles both lose. It is the first time since August 11 that the Blue Jays have lost two in a row.

Friday night brings the K.C. Royals to town. K.C. is in the midst of their own pennant race with the Oakland A's. The Royals are 3 1/2 out and are desperate to beat the Birds. The Blue Jays, meanwhile, are at home against the lowly Cleveland Indians, a team they have beat up all year. For the umpteenth

141

time this season things look bleak for the Baby Birds. But Baltimore is buoyed by the fact that Toronto lost their final game in Minnesota on Thursday night. The O's are 1 1/2 out and two down in the loss column.

One more time, with the chips down, the resilient Orioles come up with their latest, biggest wins of the season. They take two of three from the Royals, winning 5-2 on Friday night behind another strong Bob Milacki performance, and 7-5 on Saturday in front of 44,591 jubilant fans. Craig Worthington and "The Looper" both sock home runs as the Birds come back after K.C. had tied it up in the eighth. But news out of Toronto is enough to cause O's fans to throw a baseball through the television screen. The Jays sweep, winning two of the three games in extra innings. It is too much for some Oriole fans to handle. Their fairy tale heroes take two of three from a team that has to win to stay alive and the Indians can't score a lousy run in an extra-inning contest. Thank you, Cleveland. Two-and-a-half out, three in the loss column, with 11 to go.

Monday, September 18, Oriole fans are ecstatic as their old friend Mike Boddicker defeats Toronto. They are two games out.

Tuesday, September 19, Craig Worthington homers; Tim Hulett (this month's designated fairy tale hitter) also homers. Jamie Quirk, the guy let go by two teams this year, has an RBI double. The Birds seven, eight, and nine hitters knock out Detroit's Jack Morris. Bob Milacki wins his 12th, 6-2. The Birds rush to the clubhouse and their TVs. Boston is beating Toronto 4-3 in the 10th inning. One more pitch and it's over—but no! Boston miscues and blown opportunities put Toronto back in it, and they win again 6-5, their sixth straight extra-inning win.

There is nothing for the O's to do but continue to go out and try to win. They do it again on Wednesday night crushing Detroit 9-2. Mickey Tettleton is swinging free and easy again. He goes 3 for 5 and homers. Worthington continues his hot bat going 3 for 4, and the incredible Tim Hulet—4 for 6. Finally, it happens. The Blue Jays lose. For the first time in a full month the Orioles pick up a game. "I think they've played their best ball, but we've stayed right with them," says Randy Milligan. "It's got to be in the backs of their minds: 'What do we have to do to put these guys away?'" Milligan provides his own answer. "They've got to beat us down with a club. We ain't going nowhere." One down, nine games to go.

It doesn't last long. Friday night the hot Yankees come to town. They take advantage of Hurricane Hugo's wind by lifting three balls into the gale for home runs. The O's can't get the ball off the ground. They battle back to tie, but lose a heart-stopper 5-4. The Blue Jays win and things return to bleak.

Saturday, September 23, you can feel a mood change in Memorial Stadium. The crowd is no longer raucous. There is an eerie tension hanging over the huge crowd of 48,308. They know there can be no more losses combined with Blue Jay wins. This is it. The fans know that the Birds have won 15 of their last 18 with Ballard or Milacki on the mound. The rest of the staff is 5-11. Tonight it's Milacki, and every pitch is drama.

With two outs in the second inning and the bases loaded, the latest Cinderella kid, Tim Hulett, comes up with yet another clutch hit to put the Birds up 2-0. Hulett is now 5 for 5 in bases-loaded situations. The Birds were desperate for a clutch-hitter down the stretch, and presto, up pops Tim

143

Hulett once again. In the bottom of the fourth though, there is a single play that becomes a microcosm of the entire, incredible season. There are runners on first and third with one out. Steve Finley hits a slow roller to the first-base side. Stan Jefferson comes racing home from third. He slides and misses home plate. Then catcher Don Slaught misses Stan. Slaught is standing between Jefferson and the plate. Stan fakes to the right and left like Michael Jordan, dodges a tag, dips, lunges forward and touches the plate before Slaught can apply the tag. It is impossible, but it is just like the entire season. The O's go on to win 10-2 and, mercy sakes, the Brewers beat the Blue Jays! The O's are back in the race. One down, seven to go.

Sunday, the last day of the regular season at Memorial Stadium, a near capacity crowd of 51,173 throws home attendance over the 2.5 million mark for the first time in club history. Jeff Ballard loses a heartbreaker 2-0. No one is leaving the stadium after the game. They stay right in the park cheering their lungs out, hoping the Birds can carry those cheers in their hearts for the last six games on the road. "LET'S GO O'S! LET'S GO O'S!" You cannot help but think back to the last game of 1982. Moments later there is exciting news from Milwaukee. The Blue Jays lose and the Birds are still alive.

The Birds must survive one last series to get to Toronto with a chance to win the division. The bad news is they must go to Milwaukee and play the team that has just taken two out of three from the Jays and is still mathematically in the race. The other bad news is that Toronto plays last-place Detroit. The Birds can expect little help from the Tigers. It comes down to this: One win in Milwaukee assures the Birds of going to the Skydome with the division on the line. But to

144

have a realistic chance in that last series, the Orioles must either sweep Milwaukee or take two of three and pray the Tigers have one good game left in them. For one final time this season, the prospects seem unlikely.

In game one the Birds must go with Pete Harnisch, a guy they took out of the rotation two weeks ago. The always hyper Harnisch must somehow keep himself on an even keel in the most important game of his young life. The Brewers score in the first, and Oriole fans, pacing in front of their TVs, say "Uh-oh, he's going to blow up." Instead, he retires 15 of the next 16 Brewer hitters. In the third inning with two outs and no one on, Stan Jefferson doubles; Phil Bradley doubles; Tim Hulett singles, and Cal Ripken doubles. It is 3-1. Mark Williamson has the flu, but he comes in to pitch anyway, and pitches 1 2/3 innings of scoreless relief. Olson shuts the door in the ninth for his 27th save and the Birds win 5-3. Oriole fans take their first full breath in two weeks. Yes, Baltimore, there will be a Toronto series for the AL East crown. Meanwhile, in Detroit, a strange twist of fate touches the Birds. Brian Dubois, the pitcher the O's traded to the Tigers for Keith Moreland, is pitching. He gives up a two-run shot to Tony Fernandez, and that is the ball game. Jays win 2-0, although they are out-hit by the Tigers seven to four. One down, five to go.

On Tuesday night Dave Johnson is ineffective and the Birds lose 7-3. The Blue Jays are winning again in Detroit. It is the bottom of the ninth. There is one out, and the Blue Jays stopper, Tom Henke, is on the mound. Five more batters come to the plate and two of them reach on broken-bat singles. The Tigers win 4-3 and Sparky Anderson sends Frank Robinson a bill for the two broken bats.

It is all the Orioles have asked. If they can beat Milwaukee

145

in the finale, they have a chance. It sets up a situation where they can take two out of three from the Blue Jays and end the regular season tied. A coin flip has determined that if that occurs, the season will be decided in a one-game play-off in Baltimore, Maryland.

Bob Milacki will be the man who must take the last game from the Brewers to set up a storybook finish. With all he has experienced this year, it sometimes is difficult to remember that he is a rookie. Milacki admits that he is "shaking in his shoes." He's not the only one. Oriole fans are almost afraid to watch.

In the first inning Bob is pitching cautiously and nervously. He walks two; the bases are loaded, and the Oriole season is on the line one more time. Gary Sheffield is up. Milacki goes 3-2. The next pitch could be the season. Sheffield blasts a fastball deep into the right center field gap. Robinson cringes in the dugout; the hearts of Oriole fans stop, and Milacki turns to witness his fate. Mike Devereaux makes a long running catch to save three runs and possibly the Oriole season. The battle rages. No score, fifth inning. The O's get two runners on, and the struggling Mickey Tettleton is up, dropped from cleanup to sixth in the lineup tonight. On the first pitch he turns and tries a bunt to move up the runners, but fails. On the next pitch he swings away, just missing a double down the line. Next he drives a shot to deep left-center AND IT'S GONE! An unsuccessful bunt becomes a three-run Baltimore lead. Oriole fans know that when Tettleton homers the O's are 21-3. Milacki combines with Hickey and Williamson to complete a shutout and the scene is set.

Everything has fallen into place. The O's are going to Toronto to decide the division in the last three games of the season. Obviously, Toronto is in the driver's seat. They are one game up and they will have a capacity crowd screaming for them. But, of course, the O's have been in this situation many times this year. They are ready.

It is Friday, September 29. Today is emotionally different for Oriole fans than the rest of the month has been. Of course they have butterflies, gigantic butterflies, but it is no longer as agonizing as the stretch drive was to get here. It is tense, immensely exciting, nerve racking, yet exhilarating. It is 1982 again, only this time Bird fans cannot help their heroes. They can only watch from a country away.

This is the game everyone knows the Orioles must win. Their ace, Jeff Ballard (18-8), is on the mound. This is their opportunity. In addition, if they lose they will have to win three in a row to take the crown. Yes, this is it. This is the game.

When you sit down to compare the Orioles and the Blue Jays you find very little in common. They are direct opposites. The Blue Jays are loaded with talent, top to bottom, but fundamentally, they leave much to be desired. They do not run well; they consistently make mistakes like missing cut-off men. They do not "do the little things right." The Orioles, on the other hand, are woefully short in the talent category compared to the Jays. They are at the same time the best fundamental team in baseball, something a young team is not supposed to be.

Finally the hoopla is over. It's crunch time. Here we go. Phil Bradley steps to the plate to face Todd Stottlemyre. The pitch is delivered and it's smashed long and deep to left. IT'S GONE! THE FIRST PITCH IS GONE! Jeff Ballard is in an early groove. It is obvious that he is ready to pitch his finest, in this, the most important game of his career. He looks like a man on a mission. Once again the defense behind him is fantastic. Worthington makes a tough play to throw out Kelly Gruber in the second. Milligan dives to take a double away from Manny Lee. Jamie Quirk throws out Pat Borders at second on a missed hit and run. In the third, Cal Ripken throws out Wilson at second when he strays too far off the base on a ground ball. Jeff Ballard picks off another. In the fourth, Cal reaches a seemingly impossible shot up the middle. He dives, gets up, and somehow throws in time to nip Gruber. It must rank as one of the best plays of Cal's career.

Meanwhile, the Birds cannot score. In the fourth they load the bases with two outs, but Jamie Quirk grounds out. In the fifth Cal rockets a double to left center, but is not picked up. The killer comes in the top of the eighth. Joe Orsulak singles and Steve Finley comes in to run. On a hit and run Randy Milligan strokes a double, a play that Finley would have usually scored on from first. This time he must wait at second to be absolutely sure the ball will drop in, and Cal, Sr. must hold him up at third. The rally dies.

On to the bottom of the eighth and the game remains 1-0. Mookie Wilson leads off with a single and the tension is getting unbearable. Fred McGriff reaches on a fielder's choice as Mookie is forced. Frank Robinson has made the same move in this tight situation for the last four months of the season. Jeff Ballard pitches a masterpiece, and here comes "The Otter," Gregg Olson. What a spot for a rookie. This is not just any rookie, however. Gregg has not been scored on in his last 20 appearances. He has not given up a home run since April. Tom Lawless pinch-runs for McGriff. He steals second, but Olson puts down the big threat, George Bell. Lawless advances to third on the groundout.

Two outs. Kelly Gruber is at the plate. He is hitting .189 versus Olson. Olson's got him on the ropes again. He fires his wicked curve ball, and it takes a dive into the dirt. Quirk jumps up to knock it down, but can't. It rolls to the screen, and in one horrifying moment Oriole fans see their magical season flash before their eyes. It is tied 1-1. Olson goes on to retire the side and does the same in the ninth. He never allows a hit, as usual.

Much of the Oriole success this year rests on that stunning Olson curve. Now, implausibly, it takes away from them the most important game of the year. With Ballard and Olson out of the way, the end comes in the 11th. Mark Williamson has retired 25 of the last 28 batters he has faced. But he will have difficulty forgetting the Lloyd Moseby double that wins the game. In retrospect, the game is really lost when the Orioles miss on three opportunities to score in the mid and late innings. But losing on a freakish wild pitch? It is a painful way to lose the most important game of the season. Oriole fans openly cry for their "Never-Say-Die" heroes.

"Never Say Die," in fact, never had more meaning. On Saturday, with their hopes in ridiculous peril, these Orioles have not given up. Incredibly, they still think they can come back again. They have just learned that things are now even worse than they knew. Last night their starting pitcher stepped on a nail walking to his hotel room. It is the last nail in the story of the most improbable season ever. Harnisch cannot pitch, so the Birds must turn to Dave Johnson, loser of his last five games. At best you might expect total silence in the clubhouse. Instead, these guys are telling jokes. "Cleanest city in the world," pitching coach Al Jackson says, "and he goes and steps on a nail."

"Can you imagine what would have happened if this was

New York?" says Billy Ripken. "A giant block of cement would have fallen on him and killed him. I'm glad that it happened here."

Randy Milligan then comes limping into the trainer's room. "I stepped on a nail last night."

Mickey Tettleton, loosening up his arm, says, "I may have a couple of innings in me today." So much for the theory of kids cracking under the pressure of a pennant race.

Dave Johnson finds out three hours before game time that he will start. He struggles mightily in the first two innings, giving up a run in the first when George Bell singles home Mookie. In the third, Cal doubles home Phil Bradley. Randy Milligan singles home Cal, and the Birds battle back to take the lead, 2-1. In the fourth, they score again as Mike Devereaux crosses the plate on Phil Bradley's single.

Johnson seems to be getting stronger every inning, gaining confidence with each pitch. By the fifth inning, Oriole fans are back on the edge of their seats. Johnson sets down the Jays in order again in the sixth, and a national television audience wonders if there is one more fairy tale in this amazing Oriole season. In the seventh, Tim Hulett leads off with a double. He tries to go to third on a grounder to short. He is called out, but replays seem to indicate that Hulett was safe. Another potential O's run falls by the wayside.

Bottom of the eighth with the Birds still winning 3-1, "the amazing Johnson," as Bob Costas has described him, walks Nelson Liriano. He leaves the game. He gives up just two hits in seven innings and has come up with his best pitching performance in the majors in the biggest game of his life.

Frank Robinson, like he has all year, is still being careful with the arm of the Kid, Gregg Olson. Instead, he brings in Kevin Hickey. But Kevin walks Manny Lee and goes to a 2-1 count on Lloyd Moseby. Frank goes to Williamson. Moseby lays down a sacrifice bunt, and there are runners on second and third with one out. The Jays follow with a Mookie Wilson single, a Fred McGriff single, and a George Bell sacrifice fly to go ahead 4-3. After bailing out the Orioles all year, Mark Williamson will have a long winter trying to forget his last two appearances.

Oriole fans are stunned. Their incredible, impossible year is over. In a season of dramatic wins, the end would come with two dramatic losses, two agonizingly crushing defeats. Fairy tales, it seems, do not always come true.

CHAPTER THIRTEEN

The Afterglow

Time after time during the unforgettable season of 1989, the Baltimore Orioles were forced to recover from heartbreaking losses, the kind of losses that destroy many teams, especially young ones. Each time they came back more inspired, and driven. Now, within the span of two days, they have suffered two of the toughest losses that any team will ever experience.

After game two the clubhouse is quiet and subdued, but there is no wailing or gnashing of teeth. These Orioles are already recovering, already rebounding from the gut-wrenching experience of the last 24 hours. Do not misunderstand. These Orioles are not devoid of emotion. Are you kidding? They live on emotion. But the hurt is being replaced, and soon there will be less pain and more pride, pride in what they accomplished when everyone said it was impossible, pride for never giving up on themselves, pride in never giving in to what the world said was inevitable. Back in the beginning of the season *The Sporting News* polled 186 sports writers for their 1989 baseball predictions. Of these writers, 170 chose the Birds to finish last, 11 said sixth, and five weirdos picked them fifth. This is a team that has proven everyone wrong, by a long-shot. They have a right to be proud.

It was said that these kids did not understand the pressure they were supposed to be feeling. That was the only plausible explanation for their continuous ability to come through in the clutch when they were supposed to be folding. These Baby Birds, though, were totally aware of their situation. Now, they are also fully cognizant of what they accomplished within the scope of baseball history. In one season they have improved 32 1/2 games, finishing 1989 with an 87-75 record. No one has topped that turnaround since the 1945-46 Boston Red Sox, and that was due to the return of players from the war, a situation that can hardly be compared. These Orioles stayed in first place for 98 consecutive days. They spent a total of 116 days in the top spot, the most ever by a team that finished last in the previous year. They also finished with a .986 fielding percentage, again, the highest in major league history. They had a rookie reliever with a 1.69 ERA; they had the winningest left-handed pitcher in the American League, and they had a catcher with 26 home runs, despite being injured for five weeks of the year.

The statistics, however, are not the story of the 1989 Baltimore Orioles. This was a team that won despite the numbers, not because of them. They were a team that won because they would not believe they couldn't win. They were a team that developed a chemistry that may never be captured again. They were a team that lived and died on guts and emotion.

Oriole fans, a mirror of their team, are experiencing the same emotions as their heroes in the clubhouse. There is the hurt, but deeper, more lasting, is the intense pride. On Sunday these fans sit down to watch what has now become a meaningless final game of the season. In the top of the eighth, a curious event occurs. The rookie Oriole squad explodes for six hits and five runs to break the game open. Toronto fans have just finished seeing their team take the AL East crown in one of the most thrilling finishes ever. Manager Cito Gaston is preparing his team for the play-offs, but when the Birds start hitting, the fans become uneasy. Then, as the hitting attack continues, a strange sound reverberates through the antiseptic sculpture of the Skydome. The fans are booing. It is not the magnitude of, say, a Philadelphia boo; after all, these are cultured Canadians. Still, it is a boo. Oriole fans cannot comprehend the reaction.

At the same time, Oriole fans are at home pulling out their umbrellas. There is a driving rain pelting the streets, but they are on a mission. Their heroes are returning home, and these fans will be there to greet them, and let them know just where they stand. Why would an O's fan stand out in the rain for an hour and a half just so he or she could cheer a second-place baseball team? "WHY NOT?"

The team finally arrives and the cheers and yells get louder and more boisterous. "LET'S GO O'S! LET'S GO O'S!" Frank Robinson steps up to a microphone.

"In 1982 in San Francisco we finished two games out. They gave me 24 hours to get out of town. Right here we finish two games out and we get a pep rally and a parade." Yes, a parade too. On Monday, it is still raining, but the amazing O's are cheered up and down the streets of Baltimore by the amazing fans. Never has a team so inspired a

155

city. Never has a city so inspired a team.

No, the Baltimore Orioles did not win the division on the last day of September. What they did do was bring back the spirit of Baltimore, and win the hearts of never-say-die optimists across the country. They made the summer of 1989 a journey of hope for the forgotten, a time of uplifting for underdogs everywhere, and the most exciting ever for a city that has had more than its fair share of excitement. They proved that losers can become winners, and that team chemistry and fan appreciation can carry a feisty group of average players to the pinnacle of success. Their heroics will live forever in the hearts and minds of romantics everywhere.

But for those who have never experienced these feelings, all this is difficult to understand. The Baltimore Orioles have won three World Championships, six American League pennants, and eight division crowns. Ask an Oriole fan just a few years ago to choose his favorite season, however, and many will not pick 1966, 1970, or 1983. Instead they choose the year that got away, 1982. Ask someone today, and there is no hesitation. The answer will come in a flash. 1989. It was, simply, the best.

Regardless of what happens next year, or 50 years from now, no one who lived it will ever forget the incredible, impossible, amazing season of 1989.

No, some people will never understand.